*upto*speed

Photoshop CS3

The only book focused exclusively on the new features in Photoshop CS3

Ben Willmore

The Experts Agree...

"If you want to get up and running on CS3 fast, you're not going to find a better, easier, or more understandable way than the book you're holding right now. Ben has a knack for making the complex seem commonplace, and the complicated seem comical. This book should be a must-read for anyone upgrading to CS3, because not only will it all finally make sense, you'll wind up using parts of the program that would never reveal themselves any other way. Highly recommended, no matter what your Photoshop skill level!"

–Scott Kelby President, National Association of Photoshop Professionals (www.PhotoshopUser.com)

"Time is everything. When it comes to working in Photoshop, I want to make the most of my time so I can get right back out behind the camera. Despite being a beta tester for CS3, I knew, just knew that Ben would have techniques and tips that would speed up my workflow while at the same time, make my finished pieces just that more finished. Ben delivered bigtime! You want the best from your images, make the most of your time and have the best finished product, than you've got to own, and read this book!."

–Moose Peterson Author 23 books and Nikon Legend Behind the Lens (www.moosepeterson.com)

"I recommend Ben's book absolutely. It helped me understand quickly the new interface in CS3 and some things I was not aware of as a long-time Photoshop user. It is simple and clear and allows advanced users to move up to the new version quickly. Ben's books and teaching are the best in the industry. He demands and gets the highest compliment any photographer can give another —Respect."

–George DeWolfe Senior Editor, *View Camera* and *Camera Arts Magazines* (www.GeorgeDeWolfe.com)

"Not only will this book help you get up to speed, you'll find yourself excited about using tools and feature you didn't know were so easy to implement, saving you time and improving your final results. It is always a pleasure to learn so much from the masterful mind of Ben Willmore and to have such a powerful reference for my work"

–Eddie Tapp Author, *Eddie Tapp on Digital Photography* (www.EddieTapp.com)

"Learn what's new, and discover what you need to know without all the fluff. Yet another book from Ben that proves he's a true master."

–Russell Brown Senior Creative Director, Adobe Systems Incorporated (www.RussellBrown.com)

"The quickest way I get up to speed on EVERY new version of Photoshop is to talk Ben in to letting me read his Up To Speed books just before they go to press. I find them to be concise, to the point and explained in such a way that just makes sense. I wish every Photoshop book was written with the ease of Ben's books."
—*Vincent Versace* Recipient of the Computerworld Smithsonian Award (www.versacephotography.com)

"At a recent meeting of the BetterPhoto.com instructors, I offered them all a free book. All 17 instructors unanimously requested a copy of Ben's book. He's that good!"
—*Jim Miotke* Founder, www.BetterPhoto.com

"I found Up to Speed to be thorough—full of good hard cold pertinent information—and easy to read with Ben's engaging wit & humor. I really love all the nuances he includes that really help Photoshop and Bridge to run like a finely tuned engine. I encourage anyone wanting to get up to speed with CS3 to read Ben's latest."
—*Dave Montizambert* Author, *Creative Lighting Techniques for Studio Photographers* (www.Montizambert.com)

"If you want a comprehensive and easy to read update on the latest version of Photoshop, then Ben's book is the one for you. Ben's writing is clear, concise and packed with all the latest info, and his valuable personal insights. Ben is no shill, he doesn't just tell you what's new and great... if he sees a weakness he's quick to point that out as well. I've already made room on my must read-it-all list for the latest of Ben's beautifully designed, and info-packed books.
—*Taz Tally* Author, *Avoiding the Output Blues* (www.TazSeminars.com)

"You've worked with Photoshop for years. You already know the program. You don't need a refresher course. You just need to know what's new. This book is for you!"
—*Pete Bauer* Author, *Photoshop CS3 for Dummies*

"Ben's sessions at PhotoshopWorld are always standing-room only. His latest book provides ample reason as to why he's so popular. He breaks down the complex and arcane side of Photoshop into something that is understandable. And few things are more fun than becoming better at Photoshop. It's a great book."
—*Jim Workman* Publisher, *Photoshop User Magazine* (www.PhotoshopUser.com)

Adobe Photoshop CS3: Up to Speed

Ben Willmore

Peachpit Press

1249 Eighth Street
Berkeley, CA 94710
(510) 524-2178
(510) 524-2221 (fax)
Find us on the World Wide Web at: http://www.peachpit.com
Peachpit Press is a division of Pearson Education

Copyright © 2007 by Ben Willmore
Cover design: Chris Klimek, Ben Willmore, Regina Cleveland
Book design: Ben Willmore
Project Editor: Wendy Sharp
Contributing Editor: Regina Cleveland
Production & Prepress: Ben Willmore, Hilal Sala
Direct-to-plate printing: Courier Printing

Notice of rights:

All rights reserved. No part of this book may be reproduced or transmitted in any form or by any means, electronic, mechanical, photocopying, recording, or otherwise, without the prior written permission of the publisher. For information, contact Peachpit Press at permissions@peachpit.com

Notice of Liability:

The information in this book is distributed on an "As is" basis, without warranty. While every precaution has been taken in the preparation of this book, neither the author nor Peachpit Press shall have any liability to any person or entity with respect to any liability, loss, or damage caused or alleged to be caused directly or indirectly by the instructions contained in this book or by the computer software and hardware products described herein.

Trademarks

Adobe, the Adobe logo, and Photoshop are registered trademarks of Adobe Systems, Incorporated. Many of the designations used by manufacturers and sellers to distinguish their products are claimed as trademarks. Where those designations appear in this book, and Peachpit was aware of a trademark claim, the designations appear as requested by the owner of the trademark. All other product names and services identified throughout this book are used in an editorial fashion only and for the benefit of such companies with no intention of infringement of the trademark. No such use, or the use of any trade name, is intended to convey endorsement or other affiliation with this book.

ISBN-13: 978-0-321-51429-5   ISBN-10: 0-321-51429-7

9 8 7 6 5 4 3 2 1

Printed and bound in the United States of America.

Photo Credits

All of the images in this book are copyrighted by Ben Willmore, with the following exceptions:

Cover Image
Horse: ©2007
iStockphoto/winhorse
Design: Chris Klimek
Ben Willmore
Regina Cleveland

Chapter 1, Page 2
Bridge: ©2007
iStockphoto/Veni
Design:
Regina Cleveland

Chapter 2, Page 26
Woman: ©2007
iStockphoto/hidesy
Lens images: ©2007
iStockphoto
Design: Regina Cleveland

Chapter 3, Page 48
Man: ©2007
iStockphoto/Dizzo
Cylinder: ©2007 iStock-
photo/thelinke
Design: Regina Cleveland

Chapter 4, Page 58
Couple: ©2007
iStockphoto/GoGo
Design: Regina Cleveland

Chapter 5, Page 82
Elephant images:
©2007 iStockphoto
Design: Regina Cleveland

Chapter 6, Page 98
Panorama: ©2007
iStockphoto/pianoman
Bird: ©2007 iStockphoto/
Andrew_Howe
Design: Regina Cleveland

Chapter 7, Page 114
Moon Ocean: ©2007
iStockphoto/
Spectral-Design
Map: ©2007 iStockphoto/
AGraffizone
Design: Regina Cleveland

Digital Mastery Ad
Field of Heads: ©2007
iStockphoto/byllwill
Design: Regina Cleveland

Dedication:

To my mom, Dode.

*A nurturing soul who,
against her better judgment,
purchased my first Apple][
in the late 70's and sent me to
CompuCamp in the early 80's.*

*Had she not overcome
her doubts, my career
would have taken a
different turn and this
book would not exist.*

*Dode passed away on
Valentine's Day, 1984.*

To Bruce Fraser.

*A Scottish chieftain
of the digital imaging clan;
A man with a prodigious brain,
a sharp wit, and a giant heart.*

*He was our Yoda and
our own magical Merlin
all wrapped up in one.*

*Thank you, Bruce, for never
being too busy to connect the
dots for me. You are missed
in so many ways.*

*Bruce passed away on
December 16, 2006.*

Acknowledgements

I remember writing my very first seminar handbook. My editing team consisted of me, myself and the geek in the mirror. That was over a decade ago. Since then my adventures with Photoshop have put me in the path of some incredibly talented and gifted individuals, some of whom I wrangled into being a part of this book. They are:

The Queen—Regina Cleveland might as well be my outer cortex for she makes it possible for my gray matter to function properly. Had she not been a part of this project, it would have been like piloting a ship across the ocean with part of its hull missing. Regina makes it possible for me to concentrate on what's important because I know she'll handle all the details. She went way beyond the call of duty (as usual) tackling the chapter opener images as well as her usual role, which is to proof and edit every word I write.

The Peachpitters—Nancy Ruenzel, for enthusiastically supporting my idea for this book. When it comes to publishers, she's a swan in a sea of pigeons. Wendy Sharp, for her unwavering dedication to excellence and for mothering this project to its conclusion (sorry about those front teeth, Wendy). Thanks also to Hilal Sala, our favorite production coordinator, and Emily Glossbrenner of FireCrystal Communications, our indexer.

The Brain Posse— Dan Burkholder and Jeff Tranberry (My Secret Weapon at Adobe) kindly took time out of their busy lives to review chapters and technical issues with a fine-tooth comb. They didn't just provide tech editing, they challenged me to write a better book.

The Artistes—Chris Klimek for coming up with the original cover design and Regina Cleveland for updating the cover for CS3 and for her delightful chapter openers.

The Mother Ship—John Nack and the folks at Adobe who pump out exciting new versions of Photoshop about every 18 months.

The Stock Broker—The good folks at iStockphoto.com for kindly letting us run loose in their wonderful image collections.

The Parking Gods—Gary Patterson and Dave Wall for generously allowing me to park my giant bus at Liberty Coach in Stuart, Florida for many, many weeks, enabling me to settle down long enough to write this book.

And finally, to the one and only Bruce Fraser for helping me out with the CMYK conversions and pdf file creation of the original version of this book. His knowledge of color management and camera raw was unrivalled, and when it came to helping out his fellow geek, he was always unbelievably generous with his time. His passing in December, 2006 left a great, gaping hole in the universe.

About The Author

A senior engineer from NASA once said that this man gave the best technical seminar he ever attended. That same year a computer-phobic who had been struggling with Photoshop for years proclaimed that "He takes the Boogie Man out of Photoshop!" This seems to be Ben Willmore's special gift; he has an uncanny ability to connect with users of every level and mind-set; whether it's first-timers taking their first sniff of Photoshop, or razor-sharp nerds and nerdettes who are on the fast track to technical enlightenment. The common echo that Ben leaves in his wake seems to be "Aha! I finally GET Photoshop!"

Considered to be one of the all-time great Photoshop gurus, Ben is one of those guys who zooms around the world standing in front of sellout crowds while he spreads his particular brand of illumination. To date, he has personally taught over 60,000 Photoshop users on four continents. His descriptions of Curves and Channels are thought to be the best in the industry and his breakthrough teaching style of "not-just-how-but-why," is what prompted the National Association of Photoshop Professionals to induct Ben into the Photoshop Hall of Fame in 2004.

His award-winning, best-selling book, *Photoshop Studio Techniques* is said to be "Arguably, one of the best Photoshop books ever written." by Photoshop User's publisher, Jim Workman. He is co-author (with Jack Davis) of the best-seller, "*How to Wow: Photoshop for Photography*," as well as a contributing author to the *Photoshop World Dream Team* book.

Ben understands Photoshop on a genetic level. He grasps the underlying concepts no matter how difficult they seem to the rest of us, then presents them in a clear, understandable and most importantly useful way.
-**Kevin Ames**
Author, Digital Photographers Notebook
(www.amesphoto.com)

He continues to be a featured speaker at photography and publishing conferences and events worldwide, including Photoshop World, American Society of Media Photographers (ASMP), Professional Photographers Association (PPA) and the Royal Photographic Society of England. He's a member of the PhotoshopWorld Dream Team, is a PEI Photoshop All-Star, and writes for numerous digital imaging and photography publications, including a monthly column for *Photoshop User* magazine.

In 2006, Ben took his Photoshop adventures on the open road in a giant touring bus. His home/office-on-wheels has enabled him to rekindle his great passion for photography and while many of us are hitting the snooze button, Ben is likely to be prowling around in the pre-dawn hours waiting for the perfect light. His road ramblings take him all over the United States, and if you're visiting a National Park this year, don't be surprised if you happen to see Ben toting his camera gear while he looks for his next inspiration; just be sure to get up early!

To see Ben's photos from the road, and to keep track of him while he is exploring America, visit: www.WhereIsBen.com.

Table of Contents

Acknowledgements viii
About the Author ix
Introduction xii

Chapter 1   **Bridge** **2**
Where's My Stuff? 3
Interface Changes 5
Folders Panel 7
Favorites Panel 7
Filter Panel 10
Content Panel 12
Preview Panel 16
Metadata Panel 17
Photo Downloader 18
Adjusting JPEG & TIFF in Camera Raw 22
Misc. Changes 23

Chapter 2   **Camera Raw** **26**
Where's My Stuff? 27
General Changes 28
Red Eye Tool 31
Retouch Tool 33
Basic Tab 38
Parametric Curve: 41
HSL/Grayscale Tab 43
Split Toning Tab 45
Working with Presets 46
Misc. Changes 46

Chapter 3   **Interface Changes** **48**
Where's My Stuff? 49
Palette Terminology 50
Palette Basics 50
Palette Docks 52
Revised Screen Modes 54
Misc. Changes 56

Chapter 4   **Adjustments** **58**
Where's My Stuff? 59
Curves 61
Black & White 73
HDR & 32-Bit 76
Misc. Changes 78

Chapter 5   **Tools** **82**
Where's My Stuff? 83
Quick Selection Tool 84
Refine Edge Palette 86
Retouching Tools 88
Clone Source Palette 90
Misc. Changes 95

Chapter 6   **Layers** **96**
Where's My Stuff? 97
Smart Filters 97
New Blending Modes 102
Auto-Align Layers 105
Auto-Blend Layers 107

Chapter 7   **General Improvements** **114**
Where's My Stuff? 115
Device Central 116
Vanishing Point 2.0 118
Printing 121
Preferences 122
Misc. Changes 124
Extended Features 128

Index 144

Introduction

Whenever Adobe churns out a new version of Photoshop, we find ourselves scrambling to learn the latest features. Each upgrade becomes more robust than the last, making the task of learning a daunting one. You can turn to books for help, but if it's just the new features you want, the books can be more intimidating than Photoshop because they're not designed to focus on the upgrade alone. Until now, Photoshop books could be grouped into one of three categories:

1) All encompassing 'bibles' that try to cover everything.

2) Cookbooks that present the reader with brief "recipe" techniques and no in-depth coverage.

3) Books that specialize in a particular area and are very in-depth (retouching, channels, color management, etc).

So, what's missing? There isn't one book out there that caters to the user who just wants in-depth coverage of the newest features of Photoshop. If you buy the bible type book, you'll likely waste a weekend with an often frustrating and time-consuming search through hundreds of pages. Ferreting out the new stuff with the specialist books is just as maddening because they only cover a fraction of the new features, and the recipe books just skim the surface, leaving you without any true understanding of the finer points that make Photoshop's features so powerful.

Up to Speed is the first book that cuts away the fat of what you already know about Photoshop and goes right to the new features. To make your knowledge upgrade as quick and effortless as possible, I include just enough information about older features so the new ones will make sense. And unlike the sales presentations or generic overviews that come out with every new release, this book presents all the features in my signature style: intuitive, crystal clear and in-depth; everything that you need to truly get "up to speed" with the new features of Photoshop.

Who Should Read This Book

You don't have to be an expert to benefit from this book. *Up to Speed* is for all users who have a working knowledge of Photoshop CS2. However, if you're not already comfortable with the CS2 version of Photoshop, this book might not be appropriate for you. If that's the case, I recommend you read my other book, *Photoshop Studio Techniques*, which covers the most important features in Photoshop, both old and new.

How It's Organized

The last update of Photoshop made it possible to divide the first version of this book into sections that primarily focused on either the designer or the photographer. This time, however, it's not so clear cut because many of the new features reach across user boundaries and could easily be of use to multiple types of Photoshop practitioners. That said, I expect that the design/production folks won't have much interest in the Camera Raw chapter, but every other chapter should have some very useful nuggets for you regardless of where you place yourself in the digital imaging food chain.

Each chapter is organized so that you can quickly glance at the first page to get a good sense of what the chapter will cover. On the first page of each chapter you'll see a section called, "Where's My Stuff?" When Adobe moves things around, it can mess with your head, so this section tells you what to need to know about features that have either been changed, moved or eliminated to avoid getting upgrade vertigo when you start using CS3.

Keyboard commands are displayed for both Mac and Windows operating systems. Screenshots are from a Mac OS X system, but if you're a Windows user, don't worry, because even though they are cosmetically different, all the tools, palettes, menus, and dialog boxes are functionally identical.

What's Missing

Version Cue (the version management software that comes with the entire Creative Suite) is not covered here because it is beyond the objective of this book, which is to get you up to speed with Photoshop's newest features as quickly and smoothly as possible.

Also, Adobe launched an entirely new version of Photoshop called Adobe Photoshop CS3 Extended. It includes all the features of regular Photoshop CS3, plus more. "More" includes a number of features designed for more technical users (engineers, scientists, medical professionals, architects, television/film folks, etc.). They include new measurement and image analysis tools, the ability to edit 3D and motion based content, and tools for medical imaging, to mention a few. This book is intended for photographers and graphic designers (which is my area of expertise), so while I will refer to a few of the Extended features, they are (like Version Cue) beyond the scope of this book so they will not be covered in any kind of detail.

The Lowdown on CS3

This isn't the biggest upgrade in Photoshop's history, and it's not perfect by any means, but once you get a taste of it you'll quickly find yourself depending on the new features, and in many cases I predict you will absolutely fall in love with some of the new bells and whistles.

One of the updates—the new user interface which dramatically changes the way we work with palettes—might be seen as controversial enough to cause riots at PhotoshopWorld (it took me a few weeks to warm up to it, but I now enjoy the space savings it provides). Not to worry, most of the enhancements seem so natural and easy to adapt to that you'll find yourself instantly forgetting the last version of Photoshop and glomming on to the new environment like a bee to honey. Such is the case with the wonderfully revamped Bridge, the highly refined Camera Raw (with some great stuff from Lightroom thrown in), bigger and badder Curves, the new Black & White converter, and the oh-so-magical Auto-Align and Auto-Blend commands. There are definitely some features which are going to make you work a bit harder at first—such as the Quick Select tool, the Refine Edge dialog box, the Clone Source palette, and the new non-destructive Smart Filters—but once you master these features, they might end up being your personal favorites in the entire upgrade.

Whether you push a mouse, wield a stylus, or press a shutter release button for a living, there is much to enjoy and appreciate in the CS3 upgrade. While you're wandering through the maze of new features, take a moment to remember that Adobe often gives us more than at first meets the eye. That's why you'll want make sure to take the time to read through every chapter of this book (even if you've been using CS3 for awhile), because there's nothing better than getting a good surprise and hearing yourself say, "I didn't know CS3 did that!"

—Ben Willmore

Chapter 1
Bridge CS3

I F YOU THOUGHT ADOBE WOULD rest on their CS2 laurels and just throw us some chicken feed improvements, think again. The latest permutation of Bridge is one giant step toward file browser nirvana; it's faster, sleeker, and smarter. Don't let the strange new territory throw you—once you've had a chance to adapt to the new digs, you'll be well rewarded.

Below is an overview of what we'll be covering in this chapter:

- **Interface Changes:** Explore all the nooks and crannies of the redesigned Bridge interface.
- **Folders Panel:** Learn about a tiny change that can make accessing your desktop much faster.
- **Favorites Panel:** Meet the new Photographers Directory and learn how to start a meeting.
- **Filter Panel:** Learn how to narrow down a folder of images to quickly find the ones you are looking for.
- **Content Panel:** See how to organize your images into stacks or mark them as Rejects.
- **Preview Panel:** Use this panel to preview multiple images and zoom to 100% magnification.
- **Metadata Panel:** Learn your way around the new Metadata Placard.
- **Photo Downloader:** Copy, rename and apply metadata to images from a card reader.
- **Adjusting JPEG & TIFF in Camera Raw:** Quickly adjust multiple images, but be careful, there are a few "gotcha's" to look out for.
- **Misc. Changes:** The smaller, less noticeable features can make a big difference in how you work with Bridge.

Where's My Stuff?

Who rearranged the furniture?! So many things have been moved, renamed or removed in Bridge CS3, you'll definitely want to read through this section to find out what happened to all of those familiar features from Bridge CS2:

- **Light Background Interface:** Bridge CS3 has a noticeably darker background color than its CS2 predecessor. Don't like it? You can customize it by choosing **Preferences** from the **Bridge CS3** menu (Mac), or **Edit** menu (Win), clicking on the **General** category and adjusting the **Use Interface Brightness** and **Image Backdrop** settings.
- **Filter Pop-up Menu:** The pop-up menu that used to appear near the upper right corner of the Bridge window has been replaced by the new Filter panel that is found in the lower left.

Unfiltered ▼

- **Label Colors:** The colors that used to appear under the Label menu have been renamed; you can change them back by editing the settings found in the **Labels** section of the Preferences dialog box.

- **View Icons:** The view icons that used to be found in the lower right corner of the Bridge window have been replaced with icons that can be configured to your liking. Click and hold on each icon to choose the layout of panels you'd like to see when clicking the icon in the future.

- **Familiar Panels:** The Metadata and Keywords panels have been moved to the right side of the screen.

- **Metadata Panel Layout:** Adobe changed the layout of the Metadata panel so that basic camera settings appear in a layout that resembles the LCD screen of a digital camera. If you prefer the old look of this panel, turn off the **Show Metadata Placard** setting at the bottom of the Metadata section of the Preferences dialog box.

- **Workspace Settings:** A few commands that are found under the **Window>Workspace** menu have been renamed: **Lightbox** has become **Light Table**, and **Filmstrip Focus** got divided into horizontal and vertical varieties, otherwise it's all still there.

- **Find All Files:** The **Find All Files** checkbox that used to be found when choosing **Edit>Find** has been replaced by a No Folder icon that appears at the top of the new Filter panel.

- **Collections:** In Bridge, saved searches are known as Collections. In CS2, a search could be saved as a collection only after actually performing the search and clicking the Save as Collection button (which then placed the saved search into Collections in the Favorites panel). Collections is no longer available in the Favorites panel. Instead, you can save a collection directly from the **Edit>Find** dialog box where you can click the **Save as Collection** button, which will then give you the option to add the newly created collection to the Favorites panel.

- **Select Labeled & Select Unlabeled:** The **Select Labeled** and **Select Unlabeled** commands that used to be found under the **Edit** menu have been replaced by the new Filter panel. You can now click on the **No Label** choice to see all the unlabeled images (and then type **Command-A** (Mac), or **Ctrl-A** (Win) to select the images), or hold **Option** (Mac), or **Alt** (Win) and click on the **No Label** choice to view all the labeled images.

- **Apply Camera Raw Settings:** In CS2 this command was accessed via the **Edit** menu or by **Ctrl-clicking** (Mac), or **Right-clicking** (Win) on an image. That feature has been replaced with the new **Develop Settings** command, which is accessed in the same manner.

- **Camera Raw in Bridge:** The **Double-click Edits Camera Raw Settings in Bridge** preference setting has been moved from the Advanced section over to the General section.

- **View>Show Commands:** If you're used to choosing **Show All Files**, **Show Graphic Files Only**, **Show Camera Raw Files Only**, or **Show Vector Files Only** from the **Edit** menu, you'll need to get acquainted with the new Filter panel which has replaced those choices.

- **Bridge Center:** The Bridge Center that was available from the Favorites panel has been renamed Bridge Home.

- **Refresh Folder:** The folders tab in Bridge CS2 had a side menu choice to Refresh the folder view, which was useful when Bridge didn't seem to notice newly created files or folders. That command is now only available under the **View** menu in Bridge CS3.

- **Purge Central Cache:** This command used to be found under the **Tools>Cache** menu and has been moved to the Advanced section of the Preferences dialog box (which makes it harder to choose by accident).

- **Date Under Thumbnails:** The default setting in CS2 caused the file creation date to appear along with the file name under each thumbnail. That's no longer the case, but you can turn that setting back on by changing the **Additional Lines of Thumbnail Metadata** settings under the Thumbnails section of the Preferences dialog box.

- **Purge Cache for This Folder:** Adobe has simply replaced the generic term "This Folder" with the actual name of the folder being referenced.
- **Reveal Scripts in Finder:** The **Reveal Scripts in Finder** button in the General section of the Preferences dialog box has been moved to the Startup Scripts section of the same dialog box.
- **Preference Settings:** The **Do not process files larger than**, **Number of Recently Visited Folders to Display In the Look In Popup**, and **Double-click edits Camera Raw settings in Bridge settings** from the Advanced section of the Preferences dialog box have been moved to the new Thumbnails section.
- **Central & Distributed Cache:** The **Automatically Export Caches To Folders When Possible** setting found in the Advanced section of the Preferences dialog box determines where the cache will be stored. Turning the checkbox on is the same as using the old **Use Distributed Cache Files When Possible** setting and turning it off is the same as the old **Use a Centralized Cache File** setting from CS2.
- **Script Manager:** The **Script Manager** that was found under the **Bridge CS2** menu (Mac), or **Edit** menu (Win) has been replaced by the Startup Scripts section of the Preferences dialog box.

Now that you know what happened to the old, let's take a look at the new features in CS3.

Interface Changes

When you first launch Bridge CS3, the first thing you'll notice is that it looks dramatically different than the CS2 version. The changes aren't just cosmetic, there's function beneath all that new form. Let's begin by exploring the changes that were made to the overall interface so you can get comfortable before we dive into too many of the new features.

Interface Colors

The old version of Bridge featured a rather bright interface that many people found competed with their images. In Bridge CS3, they've darkened the background for both the image thumbnails area and the panels on each side of the screen. You can easily change the brightness of these areas by choosing **Preferences** from the **Bridge CS3** menu (Mac), or **Edit** menu (Win), clicking on the General section on the left side of the dialog box and then adjusting the **User Interface Brightness** and **Image Backdrop** sliders.

Appearance setting in the General preferences.

The old Bridge CS2 Interface.

The new Bridge CS3 Interface.

They've also added a **Accent Color** pop-up menu which allows you to specify the color that will be used to indicate something that is selected or active (like which folder you're viewing in the Folders panel). The default setting is System, which will use the setting that your operating system uses in other programs. Feel free to change this setting to suit your desires.

Rearranging Panels

The previous version of Bridge was limited to having the thumbnail view on the right and a set of three panels across the left edge of the Bridge window. You could drag the panel names (Folders, Favorites, etc.) to reconfigure the groupings, but you were always limited to three panels that were stacked on the left side of the thumbnail area.

Bridge CS3 defaults to having two panels on the left and two on the right with the thumbnails in the middle. Now the limitation is that you must have three columns of panels, but you can configure them anyway you'd like. The thumbnail area is even considered a panel, so you can easily reposition it by dragging the Content tab. Here are your choices when reconfiguring the panels:

- **Group Panels:** Drag the name of one tab on top of another (until you see a rectangle appear around the destination panel) to group the two tabs into a single panel. You can also **Ctrl-click** (Mac), or **Right-click** (Win) on a panel to see a list of panels. Choosing a panel from the list will move it into the grouping in which you clicked.
- **Stack Panels:** Drag the name of one tab to the top or bottom edge of a panel (until you see a horizontal highlighter bar appear) to put the tab into a new panel above or below the one you are dragging to.
- **Change Between Columns:** You can move a panel to a different column by simply dragging the tab to one of the existing panels in the destination column.
- **Collapse Column:** You can selectively hide individual columns (regardless if they are populated with panels or not) by dragging the

vertical bar that separates one column from its neighbor until it touches the vertical bar found on the edge of a neighboring column.

The center column is special because it is the only one that will remain visible if you click the double arrows that are found in the lower left corner of the Bridge window. A quick way to clear the screen of all but the center panel is to press **Tab**.

Synchronized Windows

Choosing **New Synchronized Window** from the **Window** menu will produce a new window that is identical to the one you were viewing and displays the same content. The two windows will be synchronized in that choosing an image in one window will automatically select it in the other, navigating to a different folder will do the same in the second window, etc. This might not sound all that useful until you realize that you can configure the two windows differently–changing which panels are visible as well as their size and location.

Example of a two monitor setup: thumbnails and previews are visible on the large display and all the other panels have been spread out across the other.

What makes this setup especially useful is when you work on a two monitor setup (I use a 15" laptop hooked to a 30" external display for example). You can configure one window to show only the Content panel (which displays all your thumbnail images) while another shows a large preview area. In the second window (which you might place on the smaller of your two displays), you could display the folder list, Filter panel and Metadata and Keywords panels. That way you can have a lot of room to display the thumbnails and previews and use the space on the smaller screen for features that don't need as much space.

This two monitor setup is ideal when showing images to a client. All you have to do is set up one display with a large preview image, while your second display would show the folder list and thumbnail images. Clicking on a thumbnail on your second screen would cause the screen the client is viewing to show a nice large preview clear of all the clutter from the other panels.

Now that you know how to reconfigure the panels, let's go one level deeper and look at what's waiting for you inside.

Folders Panel

Not much has changed in the Folders panel, but there is one rather nice improvement. Adobe added the Desktop to the top level of the folders list, which is the way things used to work in Photoshop CS's File Browser. This makes it much easier to drag a file from a particular folder and place it on your desktop (just be sure to hold **Option** (Mac), or **Alt** (Win) if you want to copy instead of move the file).

The Folders panel now includes the Desktop.

Favorites Panel

The Favorites panel offers some new choices, the most notable of which are Adobe Photographers Directory and Start Meeting (which provides Adobe Acrobat Connect meeting capability). Let's look at those newcomers one at a time.

Adobe Photographers Directory

This new feature allows you to search for professional photographers based on location or specialty and view their portfolio and contact information. All the photographers in the directory (over 4000 as the of this writing) have to be a member of a professional organization (like the Professional Photographers of America) to be included (there are over two dozen associations that qualify).

After performing a search, you will be presented with a list of photographers that match your criteria. Clicking on the **More Details** link will bring you to a page that contains information about the photographer's specialty and clientele, along with a portfolio of sample images. The system is pretty simple and easy to use and is an excellent and natural addition to the family of Adobe imaging services.

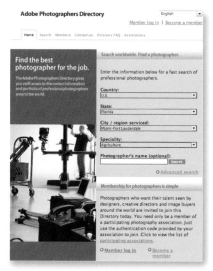

The Adobe Photographers Directory allows you to search for professional photographers in your area.

After clicking the Search button, you will be presented with a list of Photographers and their contact info.

Clicking on the More details link will bring you to a page that includes a portfolio of the photographer's work along with more information about their specialty and past clients.

Starting A Meeting From Bridge

The **Start Meeting** choice under the Favorites panel allows you to start an on-line meeting from Bridge CS3. This is simply a launching mechanism that allows you to quickly start an Acrobat Connect meeting, which will appear in a window outside of Bridge. For those of you working remotely from clients or co-workers, it's an excellent way to simultaneously review multiple images, layout ideas, etc. Be forewarned though, unless you are blessed with a high-speed internet connection, this thing can be slower than cold mud which makes this feature nearly useless (that includes you satellite users). If, however, you have the benefit of cable, DSL or similar, you might get some real benefit from this feature. Here's how it works.

The Start Meeting choice is available in the Favorites panel of Bridge CS3.

In a meeting, one participant is considered the presenter and they are allowed to share their screen with the other participants. You can also use a webcam so the participants can see the presenter and everyone can communicate via a chat window or over a teleconference. You have to pay a $39 monthly subscription to use this service (there is also a 15-day free trial available) and you can have up to 15 participants in a meeting. There is also a pro version of the service

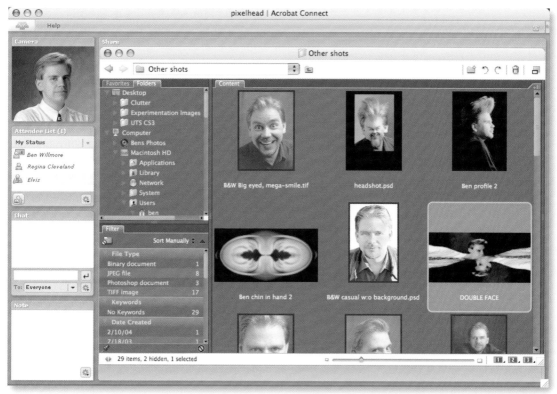

This is what it looks like when running a Acrobat Connect meeting.

which will allow multiple simultaneous meetings with up to 2500 people.

Before you can start a meeting you must first set up an account with Acrobat Connect. You can do this by clicking on Start Meeting in the Favorites panel of Bridge and following the instructions. Your new account info will be sent to you via e-mail, and it will include your Meeting URL which you can use for future meetings. To start a meet-

Clicking on Start Meeting in the Favorites panel will present you with these choices.

ing click Start Meetings again and you will be presented with the option to send e-mails to your invited participants. Their e-mails will include a link which they can click or paste into their web browsers. Through their browsers they will be able to see your screen (regardless of which program you are running). From there the presenter controls the meeting through the Acrobat Connect interface and all should go smoothly provided everybody's internet connection behaves. No additional plug-ins should be needed to use this service on most computers since the meeting uses Flash which is already installed on 97% of the computers that are used to access the internet. A nice demo is available in the Start Meeting area which will walk you through everything necessary to use the service.

Filter Panel

The new Filter panel replaces the Filter pop-up menu that used to be found in the upper right of the Bridge window. It takes up much more space than the previous version, but it's also much more powerful and informative. The improvements make it possible to quickly and intelligently search for images using criteria such as keywords, file type, orientation, etc. Let's take a look at what's available:

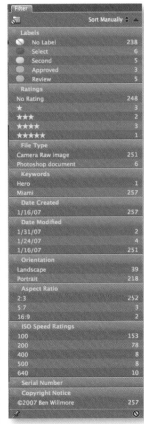

Clicking on one of the criteria options in the Filter panel will toggle the relevant filter on or off and cause Bridge to only display the images that match the criteria you've specified.

The Filter panel allows you to reduce the number of images displayed in a folder.

The choices available in the Filter panel will change each time you view a different folder because it only lists choices that would actually reduce the number of images displayed. For instance if you had a folder of images with no ratings applied, the Filter would not display Ratings as an available criteria (because it would produce no results). Other choices won't show up if all images in the folder match the criteria (such as Date Created on a folder of images that were all shot on the same day). This helps to reduce the number of filtering options available to only those that would be relevant to the images you are browsing. The disadvantage of this approach is that Bridge has to read all the metadata from all the files in the folder before it will finish populating the Filter panel with the appropriate choices.

If there are some filters that you are not interested in (such as ISO or Proportions), feel free to click the triangle that appears to the left of the filter. That will collapse that category and the Filter panel will remember your desires as you switch to other folders. Unfortunately there is no way to prevent a filter category from ever showing up.

Expanding Your Options

You can expand or narrow the filtering being applied by doing any of the following:

Add to Filter: Selecting more than one choice from within the same category (labels for instance) will expand your results and show all the files that have any of those settings (example: display all images that have either the red or yellow label applied).

And Higher: Holding **Shift** when clicking on a choice in the Ratings category will cause it to filter for that rating and above (example: display all images rated with three or more stars). If any ratings were already filtered, the above filter will be added to the one that was active before **Shift-clicking** (in other words, you can filter for one plus three and above stars).

Everything But: If you want to filter for all except one choice in a category, hold the **Option** key (Mac), or **Alt** key (Win) and double-click the choice you don't want to include (example: display images that have any ISO setting except ISO 100). The first click will select the item and the second one will deselect it while selecting all the others in that category.

Narrow Filtering: You can further narrow the range of images shown by clicking on a choice in more than one category. In that case, Bridge will only show images that match both filters (example: display images shot at ISO 100 that are in the Landscape orientation).

Include Sub-folders: With default settings, Bridge will only display images that are in the top level of the active folder. If you'd like to display and filter images that are located in sub-folders of the one you are viewing, click on the folder icon that appears just below the Filter tab (the icon will be gray when the feature is turned off and will be in color when the feature is active).

Persistent Filtering: When you switch between folders, the Filter panel will be cleared out so that your first view of the selected folder will display all the files contained within. Clicking the thumbtack icon that's found in the lower left corner of the Filter panel will cause the filter to persist between folders, so you can quickly click through multiple folders to see which images match the filtering you applied to the first folder.

Clear Filter: If you ever suspect that you're not seeing all the images in a folder (because you think a filter might be limiting the number shown), click the "NO" symbol that's found in the lower right corner of the Filter panel, or type **Option-Command-A** (Mac), or **Alt-Ctrl-A** (Win) to view all the images (which is the shortcut for clicking the icon).

Sort Order: You can also change the sort order of the thumbnail images from the **Sort** pop-up menu in the upper right of the Filter panel. The same choices are available from the **View>Sort** menu, but the pop-up menu changes so you can tell which sort order is being used with a quick glance. The arrow to the right of the **Sort** pop-up menu determines if the sort is in ascending or descending order.

Special Considerations

Now that you know how to filter the images within a folder, let's look at some specialized uses for the filters that are available in Bridge CS3:

Noise Reduction For Different ISO Settings: The amount of digital noise present in an image is partially determined by the ISO setting that was used when shooting the image. By filtering ISO Speed Ratings, you can quickly determine which images might need heavy noise reduction.

Copyright for Photo Credits: If you work with multiple photographers and need to include a photo credit next to each image you use in a layout, you can filter for individual copyrights (assuming the photographer tagged the images with this info) and then quickly copy/paste a photo credit from one image to others in your page layout program.

Multiple Shooters: If you have more than one person shooting an event and you've copied all the images into a single folder, you can filter the images based on the serial number of the camera used to shoot the image and therefore see the images from each individual camera. This is also useful when you use specialized gear like cameras modified to capture infrared light.

Video Aspect Ratios: If you work with images destined for video output, you can see which images might be appropriate for the particular format you'll be working with (like 16:9 aspect ratio images used for widescreen, high-definition video).

> **NOTE**
>
> **Limited Aspect Ratios**
> *Only the following aspect ratios are available in Bridge: 1:1, 2:3, 3:4, 4:5, 5:7, 16:9 and Panoramic. All of your images will be listed as being one of those aspect ratios even though they might not perfectly match the ratio listed.*

Vector Images: Filtering by File Type can make it easy to find vector EPS files that might be hiding within a folder that contains hundreds of pixel-based images.

Content Panel

Thumbnail images are now displayed in an area known as the Content panel. It really doesn't look any different than the previous version other than the tiny little tab at the top called Content. That tab allows you to move the Content panel to a different grouping of panels, which means it's no longer stuck in the middle of your screen.

Thumbnail Quality

If you've spent any time using Bridge in the past, and you've opened a folder containing tons of images, it's highly likely that you've experienced something similar to The Day The Earth Stood Still. When you could cook a meatloaf in the time it takes for Bridge to generate and display thumbnail images, it's no laughing matter. Adobe must have heard the wails of agony loud and clear because the process of displaying thumbnails has been dramatically improved—in some cases it's over ten times faster. That's because you now have the choice between having Bridge display the thumbnails that are built into most images (which is a really fast process), or actually opening each file and generating fresh thumbnails (which is the slow method Bridge CS2 used).

In addition, faster scrolling is possible because Bridge CS3 displays very low quality thumbnails as you scroll through them and only updates the screen with higher quality thumbnails when you pause or release the mouse button.

Quick Thumbnails

Bridge CS3 defaults to creating what are known as Quick Thumbnails. That means that it will look for any thumbnails that are already embedded within the images you browse. That will make the process of displaying thumbnail images as fast as possible.

A side effect of using Quick Thumbnails is that when you open them in Photoshop your images might look a bit different than what the thumbnail display looks like in Bridge. That's because the Quick Thumbnails are not color managed and in the case of RAW files, they were created using a different raw convertor (possibly in your camera) than Photoshop's Camera Raw. You'll have to either open the image, or have Bridge create a High Quality thumbnail (which I'll talk about in a moment) to get a color-accurate thumbnail. Quick Thumbnails will also not reflect any edits you've made in the Camera Raw dialog box (unless you use the Save button in Camera Raw to create a processed file). You'll have to generate a High Quality Thumbnail in order to get a color-accurate image that reflects what you'll see after opening an image in Photoshop.

High Quality Thumbnails

A High Quality Thumbnail is one that Bridge has created by going behind the scenes and opening each individual image in Photoshop. It will therefore reflect exactly what you should see when opening the image. High Quality Thumbnails will also reflect changes that have been made in the Camera Raw dialog box. It can take quite a while for Bridge to generate this type of thumbnail.

You can tell the type of thumbnail being displayed by looking for a border around the edge of each thumbnail image. A bold border around a thumbnail is an indication that a Quick Thumbnail is being used. If it does not sport a thick border, it's being displayed using a High Quality Thumbnail.

Left: Quick Thumbnail.
Right: High Quality Thumbnail.

I use Quick Thumbnails when I'm initially sorting my images and deciding which ones might be worth using. I then have Bridge generate High Quality Thumbnails for those images that I plan to open and edit in Photoshop.

When Creating Thumbnails Generate:

○ Quick Thumbnails
○ High Quality Thumbnails
◉ Convert To High Quality When Previewed

Do Not Process Files Larger Than: 400 MB

Previously cached files will not be affected by changes to these settings. These settings may only take effect after the cache has been purged.

Thumbnail options in the Advanced preferences.

Generating Thumbnails

The type of thumbnail that Bridge will use can be changed by choosing **Preferences** from the **Bridge** menu (Mac), or **Edit** menu (Win) and clicking on the Thumbnails section. The default setting will cause Bridge to use Quick Thumbnails up until the time that you click on a thumbnail and cause the image to appear in the Preview panel, at which time it will generate a High Quality Thumbnail.

You can also manually convert from one type of thumbnail to the other by using the **Generate Quick Thumbnail** and **Generate High Quality Thumbnail** commands which are found in the **Edit** menu. I also use those commands on the rare occasion when Bridge stubbornly refuses to generate a thumbnail for one image in a folder of hundreds of otherwise successfully previewed images. In Bridge CS2, you would have had to choose **Tools>Cache>Purge Cache for This Folder**, which would have forced it to regenerate the thumbnails for all the images in the folder (which could be time consuming and truly horrible if there were tons of images involved).

You can also use these features to compare the in-camera processing of a RAW file (as represented by the Quick Thumbnail) and Camera Raw's processing (as represented by the High Quality thumbnail).

Other Content Panel Changes

Here are a few additional features you can look forward to in the Content panel:

Drag-Select: You can now click in the empty area next to any thumbnail and drag to create a selection rectangle. All the thumbnails that are contained within the rectangle will become selected. You can also **Shift**-click in an empty area, release the mouse button and drag to create a selection rectangle. This can make it easier to select a series of images when using a Wacom graphics tablet since it can be difficult to lift the pen without moving your cursor.

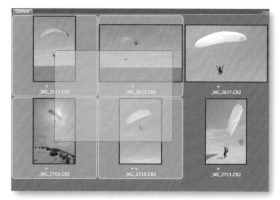

Click in an empty area between two thumbnails and drag to create a selection rectangle and select all the thumbnails that the rectangle touches.

Quick Copies: In Bridge CS2, you could select one or more images, choose **Edit>Copy**, navigate to a different folder and then choose **Edit>Paste** to copy images between folders. This is still available, but it's much faster to simply **Ctrl-click** (Mac), or **Right-click** (Win) on a selected thumbnail and choose from the options found in the **Copy to** submenu of the pop-up menu that appears (you can also access these commands from the **Edit** menu in CS3). That submenu will list all the folders you've navigated to recently.

Quick Moves: To quickly move an image to another folder (instead of copy it) you can **Ctrl-click** (Mac), or **Right-click** (Win) on a selected thumbnail which will cause a pop-up menu to appear where you can choose from the folders found in the **Move to** submenu.

Lock Files: You can now lock an image by **Ctrl-clicking** (Mac), or **Right-clicking** (Win) on a selected thumbnail and choosing **Lock Item**. This will lock the file within your operating system (using features that until now have only been accessible outside of Photoshop). Bridge will then display a lock icon above the thumbnail and warn (but not prevent) you if you attempt to move the file. If you make changes to the locked file in Photoshop, you will not be able to save the changes back into the same file without first unlocking the file (which is available from the same menu).

Color Management: You now have the option to have Bridge's thumbnails and previews match the appearance you'll get in Photoshop (and other programs that are designed to accurately display color because they use color management), or instead have them look like they would in programs that are not generally concerned about accurate color (like most word processors, web browsers and database programs which do not use color management). To access the **Enable Color Management in Bridge** setting choose **Preferences** from the **Bridge CS3** menu (Mac), or **Edit** menu (Win), and click on the Advanced section. If you ever notice the appearance of images in Bridge not matching Photoshop, this would be the area to check.

Rejecting Files

"Rejecting" a file sounds so cruel, but in fact this new feature is less harsh and more forgiving than what we normally do with unwanted files, which is to simply trash them. Through Bridge CS3, Adobe found a nice middle ground; think of it as Purgatory for those less desirable files. Pressing **Delete** (Mac), or **Backspace** (Win) now labels an image as being a "reject" (the same keystrokes would have moved them to the trash in

Bridge CS2). Rejected images can be visible or hidden by toggling the **Show Reject Files** choice from the **View** menu. When they are visible, a red "Reject" label will appear below each rejected thumbnail in the Content tab. This is useful when sorting through images and figuring out which ones you think might be worth keeping.

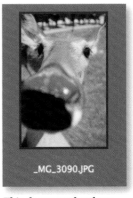

_MG_3090.JPG

This document has been labeled a Reject.

Rejecting an image will remove any star rating that was applied to the image prior to rejecting it. Reject is also a separate choice in the Ratings panel in Bridge.

All too many times, I've accidentally deleted the starting image of a multi-shot panorama or an badly exposed image that I didn't realize was part of an HDR image sequence. With the reject feature, I can now press delete, have these images disappear from the thumbnails and then easily retrieve them if I later find I made an error. To truly delete the rejected images, click the Reject option under the Ratings category of the Filter tab, choose **Edit>Select All** and then press **Command-Delete** (Mac), or **Ctrl-Backspace** (Win) to move the selected images to the trash. If you accidentally reject a file, choose a different rating from the **Label** menu while that file is selected in Bridge.

Stacks

You can now group multiple images into a stack by choosing **Stacks>Group As Stack**, or typing **Command-G** (Mac), or **Ctrl-G** (Win) when multiple images are selected. Once a series of images have been grouped into a stack, the first image thumbnail will display a double border

A collapsed Stack of seven images.

that indicates more images are hidden behind the top one, as well as a number in the corner that indicates how many images are in the stack.

To see all the images contained within a stack, either click on the number shown on top of the stack, or choose **Open Stack** from the **Stacks** menu when a stack is selected. You can also choose **Close Stack** from the same menu to collapse an expanded stack (**Expand All Stacks** and **Collapse All Stacks** commands are also available in the **Stacks** menu), or click on the number on top of the first image in the stack. If you'd like to change the image that appears when a stack is collapsed, first expand the stack, click on the image you'd like to be shown and choose **Promote to Top of Stack** from the **Stacks** menu.

The Stack shown above in its expanded state.

A collapsed stack with the top image selected (left) and the entire stack selected (right).

You'll have to be careful when working with stacks because dragging a collapsed stack to a new position will cause only the topmost image in the stack to be moved—in fact, it will

Click between the two borders to select all the images in a Stack.

pull the image out of the stack. If you'd like to move all the images contained within the stack you'll have to click between the first and second border to select the entire stack (or click twice on the number in the upper left corner of the stack). When only the top border is highlighted, the top image is selected, while both borders will become highlighted when the entire stack is selected.

I find stacks to be useful for many purposes including:

Panoramas: An expanded stack can be a nice way to keep track of multiple shots that you plan to merge into a seamless panorama. That way you know that all the images relate so you don't accidently delete one of the shots because it doesn't look compelling on its own.

Exposure Brackets: When you shoot identical images with different exposure settings (also known as a bracket), it can be nice to stack the images together and put the best exposure on the top of the stack so it's easy to figure out which image to edit in Photoshop. I usually keep these as collapsed stacks so I only see the best exposure.

Similar Shots: If you shot 15 images of the same subject matter in very similar compositions, you might consider stacking them so it's easier to scroll through a folder of images without having to see so many variations on essentially the same image. This would be especially handy for anyone dealing with large quantities of images being selected for something like a book or a catalog.

Preview Panel

The Preview panel has received some seriously wonderful changes that are not very obvious unless you know what you are looking for. Definitely take the time to try out the following two new features because they are invaluable when it comes to viewing and comparing images. You used to have to open images in Photoshop to get the level of detail and side-by-side comparison you can now achieve in Bridge.

Preview Multiple Images

You can now preview up to nine images at one time. Simply select more than one image from the Content panel and the Preview panel will show you an enlarged version of each image. When you have more than nine images selected, the Preview panel will only display the first nine. This new capability is nice when you want to quickly compare two or three images. It becomes even more meaningful for you two-monitor folks if you dedicate one screen to the preview and another to all the other panels because the side-by-side comparisons can be viewed at quite a large size, which will provide a high level of detail, making the selection process that much more informed.

Loupe View

In the photography world there is a handy little device—called a loupe—which is essentially a small lens placed over the top of a slide or photograph. It magnifies whatever is below it and is an excellent tool for evaluating the detail and sharpness of an image. Adobe has given us its digital cousin in Bridge CS3. You can click on any part of a preview image to magnify that portion of the image to 100%. Clicking a second time will close this magnified view and return the preview image to normal. You can even click and drag your mouse around the image and check the enlarged view to make sure the image is in focus and does not contain too much noise, all without having to open it in Photoshop. Just be patient because it can take a few moments for Bridge to generate the full size preview image that is necessary for this new view. That means that the magnified view will initially appear as a pixelated image which will update itself once the full resolution image has been generated.

You can also increase the magnification used for the loupe by typing **Command-+** or **Command–** (Mac), or **Ctrl-+** or **Ctrl–** (Win). The amount the image has been magnified will be displayed along with the file name below the preview image.

Selecting multiple images in the Content area will cause them to be shown at a larger size within the Preview panel. Up to nine images can be previewed at one time.

Click on any preview image to view a portion of the image at 100%. Command-click (Mac) or Ctrl-click (Win) on a second image to zoom in on it as well.

Another nice feature is that you can **zoom into** more than one of the Preview images (assuming you have more than one image selected in the Content panel) by simply clicking within one of the other previews. You can even hold **Command** (Mac), or **Ctrl** (Win) on a preview when you're zoomed into multiple preview images to move all the loupe views to the same position in each preview.

Metadata Panel

Adobe has changed the way that basic camera settings are displayed in the Metadata panel. They now appear in a layout similar to what a digital SLR camera uses. The top line displays the aperture and shutter speed settings. The second line shows the metering mode and the exposure compensation setting used. The third line shows the white balance and ISO (also known as film speed) setting. These fields will be blank if the image does not contain metadata from a digital camera. To the right of the LCD placard, the following information will be displayed: width & height in pixels, file size, resolution, color profile and mode (RGB, CMYK, etc.).

The Metadata placard.

The white balance icon will indicate one of two things:

1) The settings used on-camera if the image has not been adjusted in Camera Raw.

2) The setting used within the Camera Raw dialog box (presets or custom) and will display the As Shot icon if no change was made to the white balance setting (but it will not indicate what the camera was actually set to when that's the case).

METERING MODE ICONS		WHITE BALANCE	
Name	Icon	**Name**	Icon
Unknown/Other	[?]	As Shot	
Average		Auto	AWB
Center-weighted		Daylight	
Spot		Cloudy	
Multi-Spot		Shade	
Pattern		Tungsten	
Partial		Florescent	
Evaluative		Flash	
Multi-Spot		Custom	
Center-weighted Avg.			

If you don't like this new placard view and would like to get things back to the way they used to work in CS2, choose **Show Metadata Placard** from the side menu of the Metadata panel to toggle the feature off.

The Keywords panel has not changed in Bridge CS3, which is why you won't find a section on it here. There is also a new panel called the Inspector that we'll talk about in the Misc. Changes section (because it isn't something most people will end up using).

Okay, we've made it through the panels, and I hope you'll agree with me that though the changes were massive, things are really much more functional in their present state. We're ready to move on and if you're a photographer—amateur or professional, it doesn't matter—you should have fun with this next new feature called the Photo Downloader.

Photo Downloader

You can now have Bridge download photographs directly off a connected digital camera or storage card by choosing **File>Get Photos from Camera**.

The first time you run the Photo Downloader, you'll be asked if you want the mini-program to automatically launch each time you connect your camera or card reader (I'll use those two terms interchangeably from now on). If you'd rather not have Photo Downloader automatically launch, you can always choose it manually from the **Edit** menu in Bridge, or just turn off the **When a Camera is Connected, Launch Adobe Photo Downloader** option in the General section of the Preferences dialog box.

This dialog box will appear when you open the Photo Downloader.

These settings are found in the preferences.

Let's look at the settings available in the downloader dialog box one at a time:

Source

This is where you choose the device from which you'd like to copy images. It should automatically select the name of your camera or storage card, but you might need to change it if you have more than one card reader attached to your computer. If your device does not show up in the menu, make sure it's mounted and available from within your operating system and then choose **<Refresh List>** from the same menu.

The Adobe Photo Downloader can be accessed by choosing Get Photos from Camera from the File menu in Bridge CS3.

If you'd rather not download all the images that are stored on the card, click the Advanced Dialog button in the lower left of the dialog box and you'll be presented with thumbnail images of all the images on the card. Once the advanced version of the dialog box appears, turn off the checkboxes for the images you don't want to be copied.

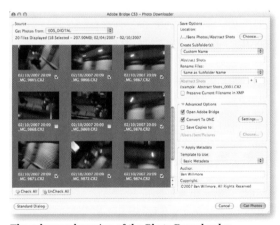

The advanced version of the Photo Downloader.

Import Settings

The Location setting determines where the images will be copied to. Click the Choose button and navigate to the drive or folder to which you'd like to place the images. You can also have the downloader make backup copies of the images by turning on the **Save Copies to** checkbox and specifying a second location. I have two identical hard drives that I use to store my photographs and this setting makes it easy to keep them both up to date with my latest photographs.

The **Create Subfolders** pop-up menu will allow you to have the downloader automatically sort your photos based on the date the images were created. I don't sort my photos this way and prefer to use the **Custom Name** setting to specify a folder name. That way I can enter both the date and the location where I was shooting ("2007|03-Miami Beach" for instance). When I use the **Custom Name** setting, I choose the base level of my photo hard drive and the downloader automatically creates a folder with the name I've specified. If you leave the menu set to **None**, it will not create a new folder and will copy the files to the exact location you've specified.

The Subfolders menu.

One new feature that I love is the ability to automatically rename the files as they are being downloaded. As we all know cameras generate names that are essentially useless, so this feature can help put some sense into your file names. You can define your file naming scheme by choosing from the **Rename Files** pop-up menu. It will automatically number the images starting with the number you

The Rename Files menu.

specify in the field to the right of the name you enter. I usually set this menu to the **Same as Subfolder Name** so my files get named with the same name I entered in the **Create Subfolders** area.

You can also store the original file name in the metadata for the file (via the **Preserve Current Filename in XMP** checkbox) so you can later retrieve that info in Bridge's Metadata panel. I don't usually have this checkbox turned on since the original names my camera provided are not useful to me.

If you plan to start sorting and editing your photographs right after downloading them from a card, do yourself a favor and turn on the **Open Adobe Bridge** checkbox. Once the copying is complete, Bridge will launch and then navigate to the folder to which the images were copied.

Converting to DNG

The **Convert to DNG** checkbox will cause the downloader to convert your photos to the DNG file format (also known as Digital Negatives) while they are being copied. The advantages of converting RAW format images to the DNG format are as follows (I would not convert JPG images because it would produce a larger file, which is the main advantage of shooting JPGs):

No XMP Files: Photoshop and Bridge are incapable of changing a RAW format image. Therefore any changes (such as keywords or Camera Raw settings) are usually contained in a separate .XMP file that is created at the time you modify the image. Lose the XMP file and you've lost those settings. Photoshop and Bridge can modify DNG files, so those XMP files are not necessary.

Embedded Previews: You can embed a preview image into a DNG file so that other software can display the preview, which will reflect the adjustments you've made in Camera Raw. When using a RAW file, other software will have to create its own preview image, which will look different than what Camera Raw would produce (since the preview was made with different software).

Smaller Files: DNG files can be saved using non-destructive compression which means that the DNG file will usually be smaller than the original uncompressed RAW file from which it was created (certain manufacturers use compression in their raw formats and therefore converting into a compressed DNG file does not ensure a smaller file size).

More Universal Support: More programs support the DNG file format than the RAW format that your camera uses (each manufacturer uses a different proprietary RAW format that is not documented whereas the DNG format is a documented standard so it's easier to write a program that supports it).

Archival Format: Since the DNG format is documented and anyone is free to implement support for it in their products, it should be easy to find software that can open DNG files long into the future. Proprietary RAW files on the other hand can be different for each camera model released which means software makers might choose not to support certain cameras because of the extra effort needed to reverse engineer each format to figure out how to support it. If the manufacturer of your camera were to go out of business then there would be less incentive to spend the time to support those formats in the future.

Now that you have an idea of why you might want to convert your RAW format images into DNG files, let's look at some of the disadvantages of converting to DNG format:

Extra Processing Time: Converting to a DNG file while downloading your images will at minimum double the amount of time it takes to process and copy the files. So, if initial copying speed is your first concern, then I wouldn't convert to DNG format in the downloader.

Can't Go Back: Once you've converted to a DNG file, you will not be able to convert the image back into its original proprietary RAW format. That is unless you use the **Embed Original Raw File** option, which will produce a file larger than the original RAW file and DNG combined and will take even longer to process and copy, which makes it a truly impractical option to use.

Can't Use Proprietary Software: The software created by your camera manufacturer (like Nikon Capture) is designed to work with their proprietary RAW format and does not support DNG files. I personally don't use my camera manufacturer's software, but who knows if they'll end up coming out with some awesome software in the future. If I convert my images to DNG, I won't be able to use their software.

Here's how I deal with the situation: I use the Photo Downloader to copy my images and do not convert them to DNG at this stage. I backup all my original RAW files to DVD so I know I can always get them back. Only after doing my initial sorting and picking the images that I think are worth opening do I convert the good images in the batch to DNG files using the Adobe DNG Converter that you can download from their web site. That way I have the original RAW files in case I want to use any proprietary software (without causing my working files to be overly huge by embedding the RAW file into a DNG). By the time I'm ready to work with the images, I've converted them into DNG files, so I don't have to deal with XMP files and I can have the advantages of smaller files and an embedded preview. Okay, that might have come across like a high-speed obstacle course, but trust me, it makes sense. Just read it again, slowly.

Now that we've covered the pros and cons of the DNG file format, let's look at the settings available when converting into the DNG file format using the Photo Downloader.

I find that the default settings are just right and will give you the best compromise between copy speed and versatility. I've done much testing and if you care to know why I like these settings, then read on, otherwise skip over this section until you see the next section heading in this chapter (Embedding Metadata). Here's how I think about each setting:

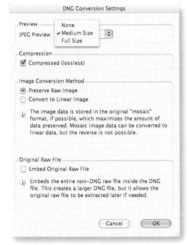

The DNG Conversion Settings.

JPEG Preview: Embedding a JPEG preview accomplishes two things: 1) It allows the software to display the preview without having to process all the raw data, which can dramatically increase the speed at which previews are displayed; 2) It allows non-Adobe software to display a preview that reflects what the image will look like when opened in Photoshop. If the image doesn't have a preview, the other software will have to create its own preview, which will look different because it was created with different software.

I like to use the Medium Size setting because the previews can be generated really fast (it barely changes the amount of time needed to copy the files using the downloader) and it barely changes the file size (a preview-less DNG file was 9.4MB, while one with a medium preview was 9.5MB). I don't use the Full Size option because it will double the amount of time it takes to download the images and it makes a more noticeable change in the file size (10.4MB with full sized thumbnail versus 9.5MB with a medium thumbnail). If the full sized thumbnail would allow me to zoom in on the image instantly, I might consider it, but it doesn't, so I don't use it.

Compression: Turning on the compression checkbox will dramatically reduce the file size of the DNG file without affecting its quality (25.5MB uncompressed versus 9.5MB uncompressed and 11.6MB for the original RAW format image). It just doesn't make sense to not compress the images because the download time also increases when you don't compress the image.

Image Conversion Method: This setting is mainly for what I'd call "RAW Geeks" who shoot with unusual cameras and use highly specialized software. The default setting will not change the general format of the data in your image, while choosing Convert to Linear image will radically alter the setup of your image (known as demosaicing) so that it is no longer contains truly raw data (raw means unprocessed). Converting into a linear DNG will just about double your download time and massively balloon the resulting file size (40MB for the linear DNG compared to 9.5MB for a "normal" DNG). There are reasons to use this setting but they are beyond the scope of this book (just google Linear DNG for details).

Embed Original Raw File: This setting will include a copy of the original raw file (so you could extract a copy of the original RAW at a later time) within the DNG file, but will not save you any space over simply having both the original RAW file and a DNG of the same file. I find it to be impractical to deal with such large file sizes, so I keep the RAW and DNG as separate files and use the RAW as my archive and the DNG as my working file.

I hope this lengthy detour into DNG-land will give you a handle on how all the DNG settings will affect your file and why I think the default settings are good choices.

Embedding Metadata

When you click on the Advanced Dialog button in the lower left of the Adobe Photo Downloader dialog box, you will be offered options for embedding Metadata in your images. This is where you can attach a copyright notice that will cause a copyright symbol to appear within the title bar of an image when it's opened in Photoshop. Whoever opens the image can then choose **Edit>File Info** to see the information you've embedded. You can also use a metadata template to embed additional information including a caption, the location, your address and more. To set up a template, choose **Create Metadata Template** from the **Tools** menu in Bridge. This metadata can later be used when performing searches within Bridge.

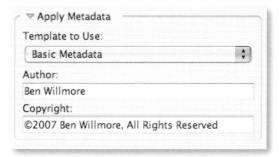

These settings are accessed by clicking the Advanced Dialog button in the downloader.

Adjusting JPEG & TIFF in Camera Raw

Bridge CS3 is able to adjust JPEG and TIFF files in the Camera Raw dialog box (which was previously only available to images that were shot in the RAW file format). This has opened such a massive can of worms that it is almost unimaginable. I honestly can't believe Adobe has released a feature with such a poorly thought out workflow. Let's dive into the worms and explore what's possible. I think you'll see that the whole setup is nothing but a disaster waiting to happen.

☑ Prefer Adobe Camera Raw for JPEG and TIFF Files

This checkbox will allow you to open JPEG and TIFF files in the Camera Raw dialog box.

A new choice has been added to the Thumbnails section of Bridge's Preferences dialog box. The **Prefer Adobe Camera Raw for JPEG and TIFF Files** checkbox will allow you to choose **File>Open in Camera Raw** when a JPEG or TIFF file is selected in Bridge. This gives you the advantage of being able to apply an extensive collection of adjustments in a single dialog box. You can then **Control-click** (Mac), or **Right-click** (Win) on an adjusted file, choose **Develop Settings>Copy Settings**, select a second group of images and choose **Paste Settings** from the same menu to apply the same settings to multiple images. That all sounds great, but there are a slew of problems that can come out of this implementation:

Double-click is Different: Choosing **File>Open in Camera Raw** will show you any changes you've previously applied in Camera Raw, but simply double-clicking the file will open the original version of the image instead! You have to go through Camera Raw to get the adjusted version of the image. That means that any actions applied to the file using Bridge's Batch command will ignore the adjustments. The only solution is to save out a new JPEG or TIFF file that reflects the changes you've made. That can be done via the Save button in Camera Raw, or by saving the image after opening it in Photoshop.

No Thumbnail Updates: Bridge's default setting for thumbnails is to create Quick Thumbnails. Quick Thumbnails are created from the thumbnail that is embedded into an image and that thumbnail is not updated when the image is adjusted using Camera Raw. That means that none of the thumbnails in Bridge will show you the result of the changes you've made in Camera Raw. The only way you can get them to update is to render High Quality Thumbnails via the Edit menu in Bridge, and as I mentioned earlier in this chapter, that can lead to dramatically longer processing times.

Changes Aren't Final: Sending an adjusted JPEG or TIFF file to someone else will produce unpredictable results. If the person who attempts to open the file happens to use Photoshop CS3 and happens to have High Quality Thumbnails turned on via Preferences (which is not the default), then they'll see a proper thumbnail, otherwise they will see the pre-adjusted version of the image. If they choose **File>Open in Camera Raw**, they will see the adjusted version of the file. If they don't use Photoshop CS3 and simply load the image into another software package (or an older version of Photoshop), they will see the unadjusted version of the image.

To get everything to work correctly you really have to be on your toes. Here's what I suggest:

If you choose to adjust JPEG and TIFF images in Camera Raw, first make sure that the **Prefer Adobe Camera Raw for JPEG and TIFF Files** preference is turned on in the Thumbnails section of the Preferences dialog box. Next, turn on the **High Quality Thumbnails** preference in the same area. Then, make sure you use the Save button in the Camera Raw dialog box to save a rendered version of the file before sending the image to anyone else to make sure they get the adjusted version of the image. Also, be sure to communicate with other Photoshop users in your organization to make sure they are aware of these problems, otherwise they might send you an adjusted JPEG file that you just happen to double-click on and end up with the un-adjusted version of the file. I honestly can't believe Adobe allowed these features to be implemented without making it easier and safer for their users.

Misc. Changes

We've explored all of the major changes made in Bridge, now it's time to examine the more subtle changes that might be difficult to find unless you really spend a lot of time looking for them. They won't necessarily all be useful to you, but scan through them because there are some sweet little gems to be found here.

Slide Show Changes

The options associated with the **View> Slideshow** feature have been expanded to include the new **Slide Show Options** dialog box (which is also accessed from the **View** menu). Let's look at each section of the dialog box:

Display Options: In this section, you can decide if you want a secondary monitor to be filled with black when running the slide show (assuming you have more than one display attached to your computer). The **Repeat Slideshow** option will simply cause the slideshow to loop when it's finished. The **Zoom Back and Forth** setting will cause Bridge to zoom into the next image and then zoom out before advancing to the next slide.

Slide Options: This is where you can choose how long each slide should appear on screen (via the Slide Duration menu), create text to appear with the image (with the Caption menu) and determine how the image should be scaled to fit the screen.

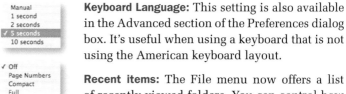

Transition Options: Over a dozen transition effects are available in this section of the dialog box. You can also choose Random to have Bridge randomly change the effect for each slide.

Click to Zoom: When playing a slide show, you can now click on the image to zoom to 100% magnification. Clicking a second time will zoom back out to the setting you've specified in the Slideshow Options dialog box.

Inspector Panel

There is a new choice available under the **Window** menu that's called **Inspector Panel**. This panel will be empty for most users, but is useful when using Adobe's Version Cue (which is beyond the scope of this book). When using Version Cue, this panel can display information about available servers, projects, and versions of selected files.

Preferences

We've talked about a few of the new Preference settings earlier in this chapter, but there are a few that we haven't explored yet. The following changes have been made to the Preferences dialog box in Bridge CS3:

Use Software Rendering: The new **Use Software Rendering** preference is available in the Advanced section of the Preferences dialog box. Turning this checkbox on will cause all image rendering in Bridge to be performed in the software instead of using your video card. This is useful when you have multiple monitors hooked up and your video card just can't keep up with Bridge's demands.

Keyboard Language: This setting is also available in the Advanced section of the Preferences dialog box. It's useful when using a keyboard that is not using the American keyboard layout.

Recent items: The File menu now offers a list of recently viewed folders. You can control how many items appear in this list in the General section of the Preferences dialog box.

Number of Recent Items to Display: 10

Startup Scripts: The new Startup Scripts section of the Preferences dialog box allows you to turn off certain features that you don't use so that Bridge can run faster. I use the settings shown below as my defaults since I do not use Version Cue, Device Central, or Adobe Stock Photos on a regular basis.

Device Central

This feature (found under the Tools menu) allows you to create and test documents for use on portable devices like cell phones. We'll discuss it in the General Improvements chapter later in this book.

DICOM Metadata

There is a new category available in the **File>File Info** dialog box. The DICOM metadata is designed to contain information about medical patients and is mainly related to features available in the Extended version of Photoshop, which is beyond the scope of this book.

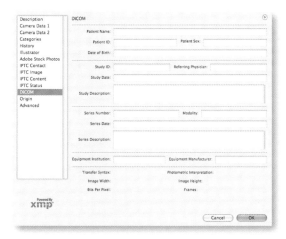

Find Options

There are two new options in the **Edit>Find** dialog box: The **Save As Collection** option is not really new, it's just been moved. This option used to only be available after performing a search. It will save the search so you can quickly perform the same search in the future. The saved collection will appear under the Favorites tab in Bridge if you turn on the **Add to Favorites** checkbox when saving it. The second new option is the **Include Non-indexed Files** choice in the Find dialog box. When it is turned on, Bridge will search all the files in the folder you specify. When it's turned off, it will only search files that Bridge has had a chance to inspect and include in its database. If you want a full search, make sure to turn the checkbox on.

There's no question that Adobe made mammoth changes to Bridge. Aside from my profuse griping about one feature (Adjusting JPEG & TIFF in Camera Raw), I am really quite impressed with this current offering. Getting used to the new Filter panel and thumbnail quality options might take you a while, and you may get a bit frustrated as you navigate the learning curve, but once you've fully embraced the new interface and all the goodies it has to offer, I predict that you will soon be wondering how you ever lived without Bridge CS3.

Chapter 2
Camera Raw 4.0

CAMERA RAW'S LATEST GROWTH SPURT has yielded a profusion of sophisticated new sliders and adjustments including the ability to edit JPEG and TIFF images. To sweeten the pot, Adobe threw in some features from Photoshop Lightroom, their new heavy-duty image processing application designed for professional photographers.

The upshot of all of this is that you can now get much more out of your images without ever having to open them in Photoshop. Here's what we'll be covering in this chapter:

- **General Changes:** This is a major revision which requires some significant brain-shifting in the way you approach Camera Raw. To get you in the right frame of mind, we'll start with an overview of some of the big picture concepts.
- **Red Eye Tool:** Remove red eye with a single click and control how much detail is retained.
- **Retouch Tool:** Non-destructively remove dust spots and other small defects.
- **Basic Tab:** Three new sliders provide a deeper level of fine control.
- **Parametric Curve:** Now you can adjust a curve even if you don't know how Curves work.
- **HSL/Grayscale Tab:** Convert to grayscale or adjust individual colors with ease.
- **Split Toning Tab:** Add color to the highlights and/or shadows of your images.
- **Working with Presets:** Quickly access custom presets of your favorite Camera Raw settings.
- **Misc. Changes:** A bunch of tiny tweaks you need to know about.

Where's My Stuff?

Let's look at what's happened to some of the features you might have used in previous versions of Photoshop:

- **Familiar Tabs:** If you're looking for the old **Adjust**, **Detail**, **Lens**, **Curve** and **Calibrate** tabs, you'll have to get used to icons instead. Adobe ran out of space to add all the new choices so they converted everything into icons (even they still use the term, "tabs") and transformed the **Adjust** tab into what is now known as the **Basic** tab.

CAMERA RAW TABS	
Name	Icon
Basic	
Tone Curve	
Detail	
Lens Corrections	
Camera Calibration	

- **Shadows Slider:** The **Shadows** slider has been renamed **Blacks** because Adobe added a new **Fill Light** slider which adjusts the shadow areas more than the old **Shadows** slider (which adjusts the absolute darkest areas).

- **Auto Checkboxes:** There is 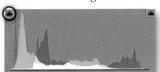 no longer separate control of the auto functionality. The four Auto checkboxes from CS2 have been replaced with a single Auto button in CS3.
- **Shadow Checkbox:** The **Shadow** checkbox that was found at the top of the Camera Raw dialog box has been replaced by a small triangle icon in the upper left corner of the histogram. Click the icon to toggle the feature. An outline around the triangle icon indicates it's active.

- **Highlight Checkbox:** This feature has been replaced by a triangle icon found in the upper right corner of the histogram.
- **Settings Pop-up Menu:** The **Settings** pop-up menu that was found directly below the histogram in CS2 has been replaced with a tiny menu icon that's found on the right edge of the Basic bar just below the tab icons.

- **Preferences from Menu:** In Photoshop CS2, you could access Camera Raw's Preferences dialog box via the Settings pop-up menu. Adobe has now dedicated an icon to the Preferences which is found at the top of the Camera Raw window.
- **Presets Pop-up Menu:** The **Presets** pop-up menu has been replaced by the **Presets** tab, which is the right-most tab found just below the histogram.
- **Save Button:** The **Save** button has simply been moved from the lower right corner to the lower left to make the space less cluttered.
- **Workflow Settings:** The settings for **Size**, **Resolution**, **Bit Depth** and **Color Space** that used to appear at the bottom of the window are now found in a dialog box that is accessed by clicking the related text that appears at the bottom of the Camera Raw window.

Adobe RGB (1998); 8 bit; 2336 by 3504 (8.2MP); 240 ppi

General Changes

Before we explore the new adjustments that are available in Camera Raw, let's take a look at some overall changes that will affect how you think about adjusting your image regardless of which tool or slider you use.

Full Screen Mode

A Full Screen icon has been added to the 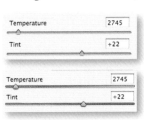 top edge of the Camera Raw dialog box, just to the left of the Histogram. Clicking the icon will toggle Full Screen mode on or off. In Full Screen mode, the Camera Raw dialog box will expand to fill your entire screen and hide its title bar to maximize the amount of space available.

In previous versions, exposure and lens information for each shot would appear in the title bar of the Camera Raw window. The title bar becomes hidden in Full Screen mode, so the exposure and lens information has been moved and now appears directly below the Histogram.

More Intuitive Sliders

Many of the sliders in Camera Raw have been changed cosmetically to give you a clue as to how they might affect an image. This is most noticeable with the White Balance sliders where you can see that moving the **Temperature** slider to the left will make an image look more blue, while moving it to the right will make the image more yellow. That should help save some brain cells from having to remember information that shouldn't be essential to understanding Photoshop.

White Balance sliders: Top: CS2. Bottom: CS3.

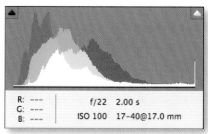

The clipping display is now found in the upper corners of the Histogram.

Revised Clipping Display

The old version of the Camera Raw dialog box featured **Shadow** and **Highlight** checkboxes that would allow you to see exactly where you were losing detail in your image. Those checkboxes have been replaced with two small triangles that appear in the upper left (for shadows) and upper right (for highlights) of the Histogram.

The triangles have multiple functions and are more versatile than the old checkboxes (although they are less obvious to the casual user). The triangles will appear black when no clipping is present in your image and will display color when the shadow (left triangle) or highlight areas (right triangle) start to become clipped. They will turn white when the highlights or shadows have been clipped all the way to solid black or white.

You can also click on the triangles to toggle a clipping display which will show you where you're losing detail within your image. A red overlay will appear wherever the highlights have been clipped, while a blue overlay will indicate shadow clipping. The highlight and

> **NOTE**
>
> **Clipping Defined**
> When an area of a grayscale photograph becomes so bright or dark that it ends up being solid white or solid black (therefore lacking detail), the area is known as being clipped to black or white.
>
> A color image is made out of three grayscale channels that represent how much red, green and blue light is used to make the image. Each of these channels can be clipped to black or white. Clipping in a single channel represents partial detail loss because the other two channels still contain detail (often referred to as saturation clipping since it's most commonly caused by increasing saturation), while clipping all three channels produces solid black or white (or total detail loss).

shadow clipping displays respond to your image in different ways. The red overlay (highlight clipping) will appear when one or more of the three colors that make up your image start to become clipped. The blue overlay (shadow clipping) will only appear in areas where all three colors that make up your image have become clipped, which indicates that an area of your image has become solid black. That's the same way the clipping display worked in older versions of Photoshop.

Adjusting JPEG and TIFF Images

In previous versions of Photoshop, you were limited to adjusting RAW format images in the Camera Raw dialog box. In Photoshop CS3, you can now adjust JPEG and TIFF images as well!

That makes it much easier to color correct and adjust dozens of images without having to resort to actions or scripting. However—as you might have already read in Chapter 1-Bridge—I have very mixed feelings about the implementation of this feature because there are some big, ugly headaches waiting to pounce on the unsuspecting user. My best advice is to read this section thoroughly, be hyper-aware whenever adjusting JPEG and TIFF images in Camera Raw, and hope that Adobe gets it right in the next version. With that said, let's continue because you can get some real benefit if you're careful.

The features available for all supported file formats are identical, but there are a few things to look out for when adjusting JPEG and TIFF files in Camera Raw.

The **Prefer Adobe Camera Raw for JPEG and TIFF Files** checkbox in the Thumbnails section of the Bridge Preferences dialog box (which is turned on by default) must be turned on in order to adjust JPEG or TIFF images in Camera Raw. With the proper preferences set, you can select any combination of JPEG, TIFF or RAW format images and choose **File>Open in Camera Raw** to adjust the files. You cannot adjust layered TIFF files using Camera Raw.

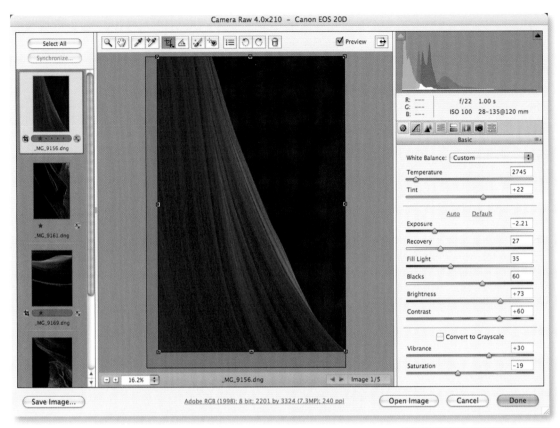

Top:
The Camera Raw dialog box.

Right:
The controls found under these three tabs have only changed cosmetically (and therefore will not be discussed in this chapter).

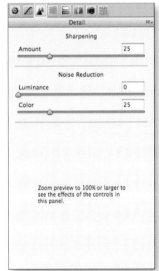

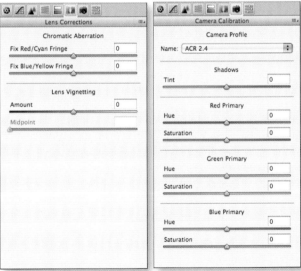

This checkbox can be accessed by choosing Preferences from the Bridge CS3 menu (Mac), or Edit menu (Win) and clicking on the Thumbnails heading.

Changes made to JPEG and TIFF files are metadata-based, which means that the actual pixels that make up the image are not changed. Instead, digital notes (metadata) are added to the file that instruct Camera Raw on how to produce the adjusted version of the image.  JPEG and TIFF files that have been adjusted with Camera Raw will be marked with an adjustment icon (circle with two tiny sliders inside) when viewed in Bridge. Double-clicking on an image that is marked with the adjustment icon will cause it to open in Camera Raw even if you don't have the proper setting turned on in Bridge's Preferences dialog box.

Opening the image using anything other than Camera Raw will produce the original unadjusted image. Read that sentence again because it's absolutely critical to your workflow. You'll have to re-save the image via the **Save Image** button in Camera Raw, or the **File>Save As** command in Photoshop to create a version of the image where the pixels that make up the image reflect the adjustments you've made in the Camera Raw dialog box. That means that you have to be VERY careful when working with JPEG or TIFF files, otherwise you might send an image to someone else and be surprised to find that they see a different result when opening the image (assuming they didn't open it through Camera Raw or Photoshop CS3) than what the image looked like in your copy of Photoshop CS3. Everything will be fine if the image is opened in Photoshop CS3, but opening the image in any non-Adobe product (as well as older versions of Adobe products) will cause the file to ignore the adjustments you made in Camera Raw.

Be sure to read Chapter 1-Bridge to learn more about working with JPEG and TIFF files in Camera Raw.

Red Eye Tool

Adobe has added a Red Eye tool to the Camera Raw dialog box that works much like the one that is built into Photoshop. To use this tool, click and drag over each affected eye to produce a rectangle that encompasses the entire red portion of the eye. When you release the mouse button, Photoshop will constrict the rectangle that was created so that it marks the area that contains red.

Original image.

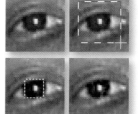

Clockwise from upper left: Original, dragging to create a rectangle, result of releasing mouse button, final image results.

If the resulting rectangle does not accurately isolate the red portion of the eye from the rest of the image, you'll have to click and drag on the edges of the rectangle to adjust its size and position (see example below).

Left: Drag. Middle: Result. Right: Adjusted result.

Options available when using the Red Eye tool.

After defining the area that contains the red eye, you can adjust the **Pupil Size** and **Darken** sliders to adjust the affected area. These settings will affect the last rectangle you defined (which will appear as a red dashed outline). To switch which rectangle is active, click within another rectangle while the **Red Eye** tool is active.

Pupil Size

The **Pupil Size** setting determines how large of an area will be adjusted. This slider can be useful when the red eye has not completely obscured the color of the iris. Using too high of a setting will remove all color from the eye and possibly cause the eyelid to lose color, while too low of a setting will leave some of the red eye visible on the edge of the pupil.

Pupil Size settings left to right: 1, 25, 50, 100 (the saturation of these images has been enhanced to make it easier to see the difference between settings)

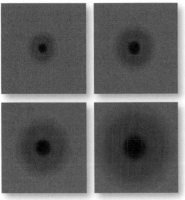

The images at the left show how the Pupil Size setting affects the area that will be adjusted compared to the rectangle that defines the problem area. Clockwise from upper left: 1, 25, 50, 100

Darken

The **Darken** slider determines how bright the iris will become. Move the slider to the left to reveal more detail in the iris or move the slider toward the right to produce a black iris. The default setting of 50 will produce an acceptable result on most images.

Darken settings left to right: 1, 25, 50, 100 (the contrast of these images has been enhanced to make it easier to see the difference between settings)

If you find the rectangles to be distracting when adjusting the **Pupil Size** and **Darken** sliders, then turn off the **Overlay** checkbox (typing **V** is a shortcut for toggling the checkbox).

If you don't like the look of an image after removing the red eye, you can prevent the **Red Eye** tool from affecting the image by removing the rectangles that define the areas that have been adjusted. You can accomplish that by clicking on the **Clear All** button, or pressing **Delete** while a rectangle is active, or **Option-clicking** (Mac), or **Alt-clicking** (Win) within a rectangle to delete the rectangle.

I prefer to use the **Red Eye** tool in Camera Raw over the one found in Photoshop's Toolbar because I can see the effects of the **Pupil Size** and **Darken** settings while I adjust the sliders. The sliders associated with the **Red Eye** tool in Photoshop on the other hand must be adjusted before you click on an image to define the area that should be adjusted. Adjusting the sliders after clicking on the image would have no effect on the area on which you have already clicked.

Retouch Tool

Adobe added a great new tool to Camera Raw that is designed for removing small defects from an image (like dust spots or scratches). To retouch an area, choose the **Retouch tool**, adjust the **Radius** setting near the top of the Camera Raw dialog box to define the size of the problem area, then align the tool's cross-hair cursor over the area and click the mouse button. If the resulting dashed red/white circle is not large enough to completely cover the area, just drag your mouse to change the size of the circle before releasing the mouse button. At that point, a second circle (colored green and white) will appear to indicate the source that the tool will use in order to repair the problem area.

> **Metadata Based Edits**
> The Retouch tool is overly simplistic because any changes you make to an image in the Camera Raw dialog box must be able to be stored as simple text in the metadata of the file being edited (so it can easily be removed later without permanently changing the image). The retouching is stored as the circle size and position of the source and destination areas, which lets it take up very little space in the file's metadata. This also allows you to copy the settings from one file to another as I'll describe in this chapter.

This tool was specifically designed for removing the dust specks that are commonly found on digital SLR camera sensors and appear as slightly out of focus dark specks on an image. Once you've determined the proper Radius setting (by retouching one speck), you can rapidly click on additional dust spots to remove them as well.

If the results don't match up with the surrounding image, then drag either one of the circles to change the area that is being retouched (via the red/white circle), or choose a different area to clone from (via the green/white circle). You can also drag the edge of either circle to change the size of both circles.

Options available when using the Retouch tool.

Top: Original image before retouching. Smaller images clockwise from upper left: Area to be retouched, Retouching circle defined, Source automatically chosen by Camera Raw, Result of auto source retouching, Manually defined source, Result of manual retouching.

1) Original image with problem area.

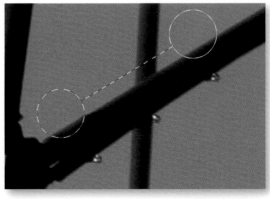

4) Dragging the green circle to an appropriate location.

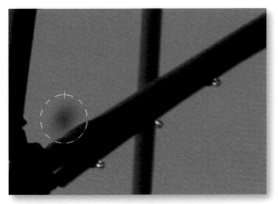

2) Clicking and dragging to define problem area.

5) Result of using smaller circle to define problem area.

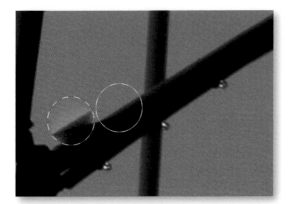

3) Camera Raw chooses an inappropriate source area.

6) Final image after circle size was adjusted.

Setting the Type pop-up menu to heal will cause the retouched area to match the brightness and color of the surrounding area, while setting it to Clone will not attempt to match its surroundings. When using the Clone setting, it's up to you to make sure that the area you are cloning from has the proper brightness and color to match the area you are attempting to retouch. When using the Heal setting, make sure the area you are cloning from has the proper texture (variation in brightness) for the area you are going to retouch. I use the Heal setting 90% of the time.

Image as it looked before retouching was performed.

Result of ten clone and six heal applications.

The edge of the photo was retouched using ten applications of the Retouch tool. The Clone setting was used to prevent the result from blending into its surroundings.

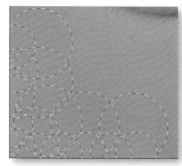

The edge retouching was blended into the surrounding image using six applications of the Retouch tool using the Heal setting.

Left: Heal setting used. Right: Clone setting used.

In the example above, I used the Clone setting to retouch the edge of the image and then used the Heal setting to blend the newly created edge into the surrounding image. By using a combination of settings, circle sizes and source locations, you can perform some fairly complex retouching in Camera Raw. While I'm glad we have this new feature, I find Photoshop's retouching tools (Healing Brush, Patch tool and Clone Stamp tool) used in conjunction with the new Clone Source palette in CS3 to be much more useful for elaborate retouching jobs.

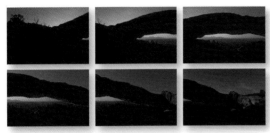

These six images were all shot within a one minute time frame. They all have spots in the exact same position (the camera's sensor was contaminated with dust).

Top: This image contains dark spots in the sky. Middle: Result of applying Retouch tool to problem areas. Bottom: Result of copying retouching to a second image via the Synchronize dialog box.

Retouching Multiple Images

When dust specks accumulate on the sensor of a digital camera, they will appear in the same location in every shot taken with the camera. To cut down on repetitive retouching work, consider retouching one image and then having Camera Raw apply the same settings to all the other affected images. To perform the same retouching on multiple images, do the following: **1)** Select all the images in Bridge and choose **Open in Camera Raw**, from the **Edit** menu, **2)** Use the **Retouch tool** to remove all the dust spots from a single image, **3)** While viewing the retouched image, click the **Select All** button, **4)** Click the **Synchronize** button, choose **Spot Removal** from the pop-up menu at the top of the dialog box and then click the **OK** button to apply the retouching to the other images. It's wise to inspect each image and look for spots that need fine-tuning because some of the retouched areas might not contain appropriate source information to produce a seamless result.

The retouching was copied from one image to another by selecting all the images in Camera Raw, and pressing the Synchronize button using the Spot Removal setting.

Left: After copying the retouching between images, some retouched areas need to be fine-tuned in the second image. Right: Result of repositioning the retouching source to match the area being retouched.

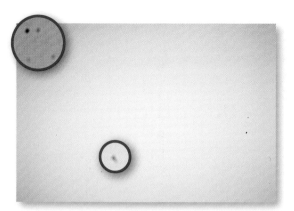

It's a good practice to shoot an "empty frame" after any important shooting session so you can see where dust has accumulated on your camera's sensor.

Cheating With A "Blank Frame"

At the end of an outdoor shooting session, I will often take an extra shot to record where the dust spots are on my camera's sensor. I do this by shooting any solid-colored, detail-free area (like a blue sky or my laptop screen when filled with white). When I do this, I set the camera to f22 or higher and set the focus distance to the shortest setting to make sure the dust isn't too out of focus (I don't want the subject I'm shooting to be in focus. I only care about the dust spots).

I then use this "blank frame" as an aid when retouching the image. In Camera Raw I'll move the **Contrast** and **Blacks** sliders all the way to the right to exaggerate any detail, move the **Saturation** slider all the way to the left to remove any color and then adjust the **Brightness** slider until I have a good view of any dust specks that might be on the sensor. I can then retouch the specks and synchronize the retouching to the other images I shot during that shooting session to remove the dust spots from all the images.

Fine-Tuning Results

After retouching multiple areas, you can see if you need to fine-tune the results by turning off the **Show Overlay** checkbox (or type **V**) to hide the circles and get a clean look at your image. If you notice a problem area, turn the checkbox back on, click on the circle that is producing an unacceptable result and adjust the position of the two circles related to that area. You can also use the bracket keys (**]** and **[**) to change the size of the active circle (which even works while the **Show Overlay** checkbox is turned off).

If you find that one of the circles is not needed, click on the circle to make it active and then press **Delete** or **Backspace**. You can also click the **Clear All** button to remove all the retouching circles and start over.

The retouched areas will interactively change to reflect any changes you make to the adjustment sliders in Camera Raw. I often take advantage of this when performing retouching by first darkening the image to make it easier to see dust spots in bright areas (such as the sky) and then brightening the image to reveal problems in the darker areas of the image. It's much better to deal with all the dust specks at the beginning of your workflow rather than finding them in more disagreeable ways: after you've made a huge print of the image, after you've sent it to a client, etc.

Making It Permanent

Clicking the **Done** button in Camera Raw will record the retouching you've applied into the metadata of the image (as simple text attached to the file). You'll still be able to fine-tune your results when you re-open the image in Camera Raw (it just reads the metadata which contains the size and position of each of the retouching circles without permanently applying the changes). To make the changes permanent, you'll have to save a new version of the image by clicking the **Save Image** button in Camera Raw, or saving the image after opening it in Photoshop.

Now that you've been introduced to the new retouching tools, let's explore the wonderful array of new adjustments available in Camera Raw 4.0.

Basic Tab

Photoshop CS2's Adjust tab has been transformed into the new Basic tab, with an icon that resembles a lens aperture and many new features.

If you're comfortable with the previous incarnation of Camera Raw, the first thing you might notice is the lack of the familiar **Shadows** slider. Adobe has simply renamed that slider **Blacks** to more accurately reflect its purpose and to prevent confusion with the new **Fill Light** slider, which will affect dark areas (often referred to as shadows). Since there have been quite a few changes, let's take a look at all of the basic tonal adjustments (both new and old) found under the Basic tab so you can get a sense for how to use them as a whole.

There are a total of four sliders that control the brightness of your image (**Exposure**, **Recovery**, **Fill Light**, and **Blacks**). This can cause confusion until you realize that each one concentrates its adjustment on a different brightness range within the image, and together provide a much simpler approach then having to use the myriad of choices found in Photoshop.

Exposure: This slider determines the brightness level of the brightest area of your image. Moving the slider toward the right will brighten your image, while moving it to the left will darken it. This slider will affect the entire brightness range in your image, but when using it, you should focus on the brightest areas because that's what the slider is concentrating on.

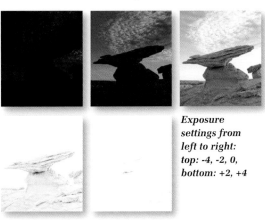

Exposure settings from left to right: top: -4, -2, 0, bottom: +2, +4

Recovery: This slider allows you to recover lost detail caused by in-camera overexposure or overly aggressive adjustment of the Exposure slider. Moving the Recovery slider toward the right will darken the brightest areas of your image. This slider is very useful when the default settings in Camera Raw cause the highlights within the image to lose detail.

> **NOTE**
>
> **JPEG versus RAW**
> Most digital SLR cameras capture 4096 brightness levels. Shooting in RAW format will retain all those brightness levels which allows for greater recovery of detail from the highlights of an image when compared to a JPEG file (which contains only 256 brightness levels), and discards partially clipped highlight detail to obtain a smaller file.

Left: Original image. Middle: Clouds darkened by setting Recovery to +50. Right: Attempting to darken the clouds by adjusting the Exposure slider.

Fill Light: This slider controls the brightness of areas that are a little brighter than black. You might generically call these areas the "shadows" (which is why Adobe renamed the old **Shadows** slider to **Blacks** since it controls only the absolutely darkest areas of the image). Moving the slider toward the right will brighten shadow areas to make it possible to see any detail that might be lurking in those areas.

Left: Original image. Middle: Horse lightened by setting Fill Light to +50. Right: Attempting to brighten the horse by maxing out the Brightness slider at +150 (the Blacks slider was already set to its lowest setting).

Blacks: This slider determines how dark the darkest area of your image will become. Moving the slider toward the right will darken that area, while moving it to the left will lighten it. I usually adjust the **Blacks** slider before adjusting the **Fill Light** slider and will often fine-tune the **Blacks** slider afterward.

Blacks settings from left to right: Zero, 50, 100.

Brightness: This slider controls the overall brightness of your image by concentrating its adjustment on the middle brightness range within your image. The **Exposure** slider will determine if any areas will appear as white, while the **Blacks** slider will determine if any areas will be black.

Brightness settings from left to right: -150, 0, +150.

Contrast: This slider controls the separation between bright and dark areas. As you move it toward the right, bright areas will become brighter and dark areas will become darker to exaggerate their differences. Moving the slider to the left will make bright and dark areas more similar, lessening their differences.

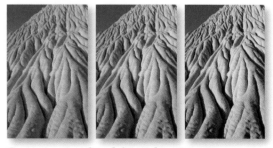

Contrast settings from left to right: -50, 0, +50.

Now that we've covered the tonal adjustments available under the Basic tab, let's take a look at two often confused controls that dictate the level of color in your image: Vibrance and Saturation.

Left: Original image. Middle: Vibrancy increased by 45. Right: Saturation increased by 45 instead.

Vibrance: Moving this slider toward the right will make your image more colorful, but will concentrate the change disproportionately to the colors that are not all that saturated to begin with. It will also prevent skin tones from becoming overly saturated in the process (although that might also cause it to prevent certain earth tones from reaching their full potential).

Saturation: Moving this slider toward the right will make all the colors within your image more colorful. It will adjust all areas an equal amount, which has the consequence of causing some colors to become overly saturated before others reach their full potential (which is why the **Vibrance** slider is often a better choice).

Left: Original image. Right: Emphasizing subtle colors with +100 Vibrancy and -35 Saturation.

Moving the Vibrance and Saturation sliders in opposite directions can help to change the relationship between subtle and saturated colors in an image. To de-emphasize the subtle colors in an image, move the Vibrance slider all the way to the left, then adjust the Saturation slider to control the overall color in your image.

Left: Original image. Right: De-emphasizing subtle colors with -100 Vibrancy and +100 Saturation.

To emphasize the more subtle colors in an image, set the Vibrance slider all the way to the right and use the Saturation slider to control the overall color in your image.

Convert to Grayscale: This checkbox will remove all color from the document to produce a grayscale image. The results are not the same as moving the **Vibrance** and **Saturation** sliders all the way to the left (which would also produce a grayscale image). Instead, this checkbox invokes the **Convert to Grayscale** checkbox that is found under the HSL/Grayscale tab which will usually produce a better looking grayscale image than is achieved by lowering the **Vibrance** and **Saturation** sliders. Adobe has simply positioned the checkbox near the Vibrance and Saturation sliders so you won't be tempted to use those sliders when you want a black and white image. We'll talk about the adjustments available when converting to grayscale later in this chapter.

Now that you've seen what's available under the Basic tab, let's get into the other tabs in Camera Raw 4.0.

Parametric Curve

A new method for adjusting a curve has been added under the Tone Curve tab in Camera Raw. It's called a Para-metric curve and is in addition to the standard Point curve that was available in previous versions. The Parametric curve offers four sliders that control the shape of the curve that will be applied to your image. You can think of these four sliders as a potential replacement for the Brightness slider that is found under the Basic tab.

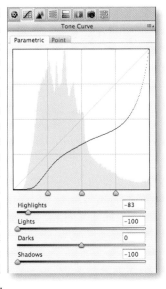

Top: Original image. Bottom: Result of applying the Parametric Curve shown at left.

Highlights: Brightens or darkens the brightest areas of your image and slowly tapers off once it gets into the areas that are approximately 40% gray. You can control the general brightness range that this slider affects by moving the slider that appears near the bottom right edge of the curve.

Lights: Brightens or darkens the middle brightness range with a slight preference for the brighter areas of the image.

Darks: Brightens or darkens the middle brightness range with a slight preference for the darker areas of the image.

The middle slider found at the bottom edge of the curve determines the brightness level that will separate the **Lights** slider from the **Darks** slider. This slider can be used to control what Camera Raw considers to be the separation point between light and dark areas of your image. You might consider replacing the Brightness slider that is found under the Basic tab with the **Lights** and **Darks** sliders since they offer you more control over the overall brightness of your image.

Shadows: Brightens or darkens the darkest areas of your image and slowly tapers off once it gets into the areas that are approximately 60% gray. You can control the general brightness range that this slider affects by moving the slider that appears near the bottom left edge of the curve.

I occasionally use the Parametric curve to add contrast in dark or bright areas of an image. To add contrast to the dark areas of an image, move the Shadows slider to the left and the Darks slider toward the right and then adjust the slider that appears near the bottom left of the curve to control which brightness range is affected. To add contrast to the bright areas of an image, move the Highlights slider toward the right and the Lights slider toward the left.

Working With Adobe Photoshop Lightroom

Adobe recently released **Adobe Photoshop Lightroom,** a stand-alone application (not included with Photoshop in spite of its shared name) which is designed for cataloging and adjusting a photographer's image library. The adjustment engine that is used behind the scenes in **Lightroom** is a variant of the **Camera Raw** dialog box that is found in **Photoshop**. Because the two programs share the same adjustment engine, it is possible to adjust an image in either program and have the changes honored in both of them. This doesn't happen automatically, but with a few changes and some careful footwork, you should be able to get both applications to cooperate.

The first step is to get the two programs to either use DNG files (which can incorporate image adjustment settings and the raw image data in a single file), or have Lightroom write its adjustments into an XMP file just like Camera Raw does (by default, Lightroom saves the adjustments in its database, which Camera Raw cannot access). To save image adjustments into a Camera Raw friendly XMP file, choose **Preferences** from the **Lightroom** menu (Mac), or **Edit** menu (Win), click on the **File Management** tab, and turn on the **Automatically write changes into XMP** checkbox within **Lightroom**.

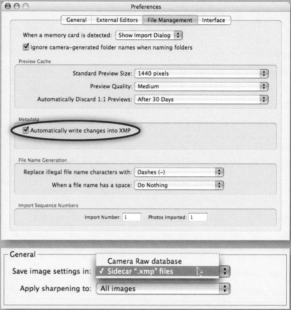

The next step is to make sure that **Camera Raw** is set to write its adjustments into an XMP file so that **Lightroom** can use them (that's the default setting, but it's good to double check). Choose **Camera Raw Preferences** from the **Bridge CS3** menu (Mac), or **Edit** menu (Win) within **Bridge** and make sure the **Save image settings in** pop-up menu is set to **Sidecar ".xmp" files**.

Once both programs are set to store their adjustments in .XMP files, you are free to adjust your images in either application. **Camera Raw** will read the XMP file associated with the RAW image and therefore will use the last adjustment applied to the image regardless of which program was used to make the changes.

When viewing images in **Lightroom**, an exclamation mark icon will appear in the upper right of an image's thumbnail when the image has been modified outside of **Lightroom.** Clicking the icon will cause **Lightroom** to prompt you with the dialog box shown here. Clicking the **Import Settings from Disk** button will cause **Lightroom** to honor any changes made to the image in **Camera Raw**, while clicking the **Overwrite Settings** button will cause the last adjustments applied in **Lightroom** to be used instead. You can always click the **Do Nothing** button to leave the image in its current state (complete with exclamation icon) so you can decide how to deal with the image at a later date.

I have completely replaced **Bridge** and **Camera Raw** with **Lightroom** because I find it to be a much more efficient way to perform initial adjustments on my images. **Lightroom** also has the capability to catalog your entire library of photographs and has many interface refinements that are not available in **Camera Raw**.

Left: Original image. Right: Contrast was added to the dark areas of the image by lowering the Shadows setting and increasing the Darks setting.

If you know how to use the normal version of Curves (known as the Point Curve in Camera Raw), then the Parametric Curve might seem like a huge step backward. Everything that can be done with the Parametric Curve—and a heck of a lot more—can be done with a lot more precision and flexibility using the Point Curve. As a passionate user of Photoshop's Curves dialog box, I find using the Parametric Curve to be about as frustrating as trying to breathe underwater. Having said that, the Parametric Curve is a useful stepping stone between the Brightness slider found under the Basic tab and the full-fledged Point Curve, so it shouldn't be ignored by those who are not comfortable working with the Point Curve.

> **(NOTE)**
>
> **Learning Curves**
> *The general concept of Curves is covered in greater detail in **Chapter 4–Adjustments**. For a more in-depth description of how to use the **Point Curve**, refer to the **Understanding Curves** chapter of my **Photoshop CS3 Studio Techniques** book.*

HSL/Grayscale Tab

The new HSL/Grayscale tab will allow you to independently adjust eight colors within your image. Once you click on this tab, you can choose between adjusting the Hue (basic color), Saturation (how colorful) and Luminance (how bright) of each of the listed colors. Unlike Photoshop's Hue/Saturation dialog box, the sliders found in Camera Raw allow you to adjust Oranges, Aquas and Purples. This allows more control over each individual color within your image and allows you to have more control over greenery (which is often more yellow than green) and skin tones than what you can accomplish in Photoshop.

Left: Original image. Right: Reds and Yellows were saturated, greens were desaturated and made darker.

I use these sliders to fine-tune the color in my images. Here are a few examples of where I've found them to be useful: **1)** Adjust the Yellows slider under the Hue tab to make greenery less yellow and more green (I also often lower the saturation), **2)** Darken blue skies and fine-tune the color of the sky using the Blues, Aquas, or Purples sliders, **3)** Lower the Saturation and Luminance of distracting background elements to force the eye to look at the subject of a photograph.

Converting to Grayscale

Turning on the **Convert to Grayscale** checkbox under the HSL/Grayscale tab will cause Camera Raw to remove all color from your image and present you with eight sliders that will control the brightness of different areas of your image.

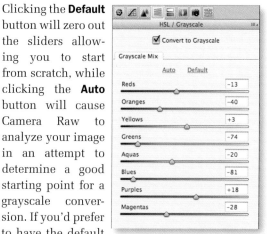

Clicking the **Default** button will zero out the sliders allowing you to start from scratch, while clicking the **Auto** button will cause Camera Raw to analyze your image in an attempt to determine a good starting point for a grayscale conversion. If you'd prefer to have the default setting start with all the sliders zeroed out, choose **Camera Raw Preferences** from the **Bridge CS3** menu (Mac), or **Edit** menu (Win) and turn off the **Apply auto grayscale mix when converting to grayscale** checkbox.

☑ Apply auto grayscale mix when converting to grayscale

This checkbox can be found in the Camera Raw Preferences dialog box.

Top left: Original image.
Top right:
Result of moving Saturation slider all the way to the left.
Middle left:
Converted to grayscale with default settings.
Middle right:
Converted to grayscale using Auto.
Bottom:
Converted with custom settings shown at left.

Split Toning Tab

The Split Toning tab allows you to force color into the brightest and darkest areas of your image. The Hue slider determines the color that will be used, while the Saturation slider determines how strong the color will be. The Balance slider controls the separation between highlights and shadows. Moving the slider toward the left will cause the Shadows sliders to affect a wider range of brightness levels, while moving it to the right will cause the Highlights sliders to affect a wider brightness range.

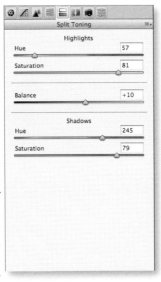

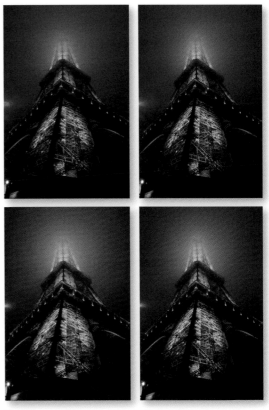

Balance clockwise from upper left: -100, -50, 50, 100.

You can also use the Split Toning feature in an attempt to correct for different lighting conditions in the highlights and shadows of an image. In the example below, the dark portion of the image looked blue after adjusting the White Balance for the bright area of the image. The blue was toned down by adding its opposite color (yellow) to the shadow areas.

Left: Original image. Right: Yellow was added to the highlights and blue/purple was added to the shadows using the settings shown above.

Left: Original image. Right: Yellow was added to the highlights and blue/purple was added to the shadows using the settings shown above.

Working with Presets

You can now save a collection of Camera Raw settings as a preset and then easily apply them to any image in the future.

To save a preset, click the **New Preset** icon (it looks like a sheet of paper with the corner turned up) at the bottom of the Presets tab. The dialog box that appears will allow you to specify a name and choose which settings will be included in the preset.

Once you've saved a preset, you can quickly apply it to the selected image in Camera Raw by clicking on its name under the Presets tab, or by choosing its name from the **Apply Presets** submenu from the side menu (accessed by clicking the small icon that appears to the right of the name of the active tab) in Camera Raw.

To delete a preset, click on the name of the preset and click the **Trash Can** icon at the bottom of the Presets list.

This dialog box will appear when you click on the New Preset icon at the bottom of the Presets tab panel.

Each preset is saved as an .XMP file in a special folder on your hard drive. Perform a search on your drive for one of the preset names to find the location of the folder (the path is too long to be usefully listed here). If you need to copy the presets from one computer to another, just copy the folder that contains the .XMP files to the same location on the second machine.

Misc. Changes

Now let's explore the more subtle, hard-to-find changes in the Camera Raw dialog box.

P for Preview: You can now type **P** to toggle the preview checkbox that's found at the top of the Camera Raw dialog box. As with previous versions, this checkbox only toggles the preview for the currently active adjustment tab. If you want to see the collective difference of all the tabs, switch between the **Image Settings** (for the before version) and **Custom Settings** (for the after version) from the side menu found to the right of the currently active tab name.

Open as Smart Object: You can now specify that images adjusted within Camera Raw should be opened as Smart Objects by clicking on the workflow settings that appear below your image and turning on the **Open in Photoshop as Smart Objects** checkbox. That will cause the **Open Image** button near the bottom right of the Camera Raw dialog box to be re-labeled **Open Object**.

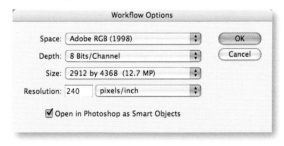

Once you've opened an image via the **Open Object** button, you can choose **Layer>Smart Objects>New Smart Object via Copy** to create an identical layer that can be adjusted using different Camera Raw settings. Double-click on the thumbnail image for the layer (within Photoshop's Layers palette) to access the Camera Raw dialog box. Once you have multiple layers with different Camera Raw settings applied, you can add a Layer Mask to each layer and then hide areas of the top layer to reveal the alternative Camera Raw settings that were used on the layer below.

This technique is very useful when the sky in an image would benefit from different Camera Raw settings than those used for the rest of the image.

Update DNG Previews: You now have the option of updating the JPEG preview that is embedded within DNG files. After updating the DNG preview to reflect the changes you've made in the Camera Raw dialog box, those changes will be reflected in the preview that is shown in programs like Microsoft iView or Extensis Portfolio. To update the embedded preview, choose **Update DNG Previews** from the side menu of the Camera Raw dialog box.

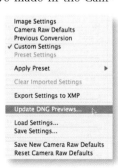

> **NOTE**
>
> **Dumb Objects?**
>
> *Just because you've opened an image as a Smart Object does not mean that Photoshop will become easier to use. It's very easy to accidentally choose the wrong command and really mess up your workflow.*
>
> *Choosing **Layer> Duplicate Layer** when a Smart Object is active will produce an identical layer that will always share the Camera Raw settings of its parent. Making changes to either layer's Camera Raw settings will cause both layers to update.*
>
> *Choosing **Layer>Smart Objects>Convert to Smart Object** will embed the active Smart Object within another, which will prevent you from being able to double-click on the layer to access the Camera Raw settings that produced the image.*

This update to Camera Raw is reflective of Adobe's deep commitment to the professional photography community (the features snagged from the new Photoshop Lightroom are a testament to that), but that doesn't mean that amateurs can't enjoy the new offering as well. For some, this update will make it possible to process their images, start-to-finish, without ever once opening Photoshop. There's a great deal to absorb, and it might take some rethinking when it comes to establishing a comfortable workflow in this new environment. At first glance, some of the adjustments might seem so similar as to appear nearly identical (and redundant), but once you've tested out all of the new goodies with a wide variety of images, I believe you'll really appreciate the nuances, and ultimately find a combination of tools that will significantly enhance your experience with Camera Raw.

Chapter 3
Interface Changes

THE WAY YOU WORK AND interact with palettes has changed dramatically in CS3. The new arrangement will take some getting used to, and while some folks love the latest bells and whistles, others are practically in mourning. If you find yourself having separation anxiety, don't fret too much; you can get some of the old stuff back.

The most radical change made to palettes in CS3 is that they can now be grouped into Docks that cling to the edge of your screen, and each palette can be collapsed down into an icon that can be clicked to expand or collapse the palette.

Below is an overview of what we'll be covering in this chapter:

- **Palette Terminology:** There are so many terms associated with palettes these days (minimized, docked, collapsed, grouped, etc.) I thought it important to start out by defining the differences between them, so that we are all speaking the same language.
- **Palette Basics:** You'll get a primer on the basics of palettes which covers the subtle but important changes that were made, and you'll find out how to interact with the palettes.
- **Palette Docks:** Learn to store palettes in a dock and quickly access them when needed.
- **Revised Screen Modes:** Learn about the new Maximized Screen Mode and other changes.
- **Misc. Changes:** A few tweaks that might affect the way you approach Photoshop.

Where's My Stuff?

Let's look at what's happened to some of the features you might have used in previous versions of Photoshop:

- **Two-column Toolbar:** Adobe has changed the default settings to give you a brand new, single-column Toolbar. To get back to the two-column layout you know and love, just click the tiny double arrows that appear in the upper left corner of the Toolbar.
- **Palette Well:** Photoshop CS2 offered a Palette Well along the right side of the Options bar. This feature is no longer available in CS3 and there's no way to get it back.

- **Palette Stacks:** You used to be able to drag the name of one palette to the top or bottom edge of another palette to stack them together. That would allow you to move the palettes as a group and still see the full contents of both. This feature has been replaced by the new palette docks in Photoshop CS3. We'll talk about them in detail in this chapter.

■ **Palette Menus:** The icon used to access the side menus for all the palettes has changed. It used to  look like a triangle inside of a circle, and now it looks like three tiny horizontal lines with an itsy-bitsy down-pointing triangle next to it. You have the same choices as the old menus though. They only changed the look of the icons used to access the menus.

Palette Terminology

Let's talk about a little terminology, otherwise you might get mixed up when reading about all the new features. If you already know the difference between all the terms listed below, feel free to skip over them and jump right into the new features starting with Palette Basics. Here are the general terms and what they mean:

Palette: A palette is everything that's found under the Window menu, with the exception of Tools and Options, which I consider to be "bars" because they can't be resized, grouped with the palettes, collapsed down to an icon and when you press Shift-Tab they are the only things that doesn't go away (pressing Tab will hide both the bars and palettes). You'll see that I refer to them as the Toolbar or Options bar.

Group: A palette that contains more than one tab at the top is actually a group of more than one palette. The tab that includes an "X" on its right edge (which is used for closing the tab) and is the lightest in the group

NOTE

Palette or Group?
I'll refer to a Group as a Palette when the feature I'm talking about can work on either a single palette or a group of palettes.

determines which palette settings will be visible in the group. If you want to work on an individual palette, you'll have to do something to the tab that contains the palette's name. If you want to move the entire palette group, you'll have to do something with the horizontal bar that appears above the tabs.

Dock: A Dock is a dark gray container that is stuck to the edge of your screen, and it can hold one or more palettes stacked one on top of the other. This is the replacement for the CS2 Palette Well. I'll explain how to use docks and their icons later in this chapter.

Dock Icon: Any palette that is stored in a dock can be collapsed into an icon which will get it out of the way until you want to expand it and use its features.

Snap: When you move a palette very close to the edge of your screen it will be pulled (as if it got too close to a vacuum) to precisely align with the edge of your screen. This is known as snapping.

NOTE

Prevent Snapping
Hold the Control key when moving a palette to prevent it from snapping to the screen edge.

Minimize: A palette can be minimized so that you can only see the tabs that it contains, and easily restored later to reveal its content. This is especially useful when a palette is snapped to the bottom of your screen because you can restore it and minimize it and the palette remains placed at the bottom of the screen.

Palette Basics

Now that we're all speaking the same palette-babble, let's take a look at some of the basic functionality and how some of the palette operations have changed in Photoshop CS3.

Finding The Palettes

All the palettes available in Photoshop are listed under the **Window** menu. In Photoshop CS2, you would find a dash mark next to any palettes that were partially or fully obscured by another palette. In Photoshop CS3, partially obscured palettes are simply listed as not active (no checkmark next to them).

The Window menu in CS3.

Re-sizing A Palette

Unfortunately, with CS3 we lose the ability to quickly resize a palette with a single click because the maximize icon has been removed. I miss that functionality for those times when I want the Layers palette to expand and become just large enough to display all the layers in the active document. Adobe made up for that omission by adding a bunch of new ways to resize a palette.

In previous versions of Photoshop, you had to drag the lower right corner of a palette to change its size. In CS3 you can drag from any corner or edge

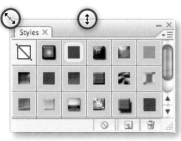

To re-size a palette, move close to the edge of a palette and watch for arrows.

of the palette. Just look for feedback icons (they look like double arrows) that indicate you're in the right position to start re-sizing the palette. This is really helpful when a palette is docked with others or snapped to the bottom of your screen (you no longer have to move the palette up, resize it and then snap it back to the bottom of your screen as you did in CS2).

Repositioning Palettes

To reposition a group of palettes, drag the horizontal bar that appears above the palette tabs. You can now drag that bar to the bar on another group of palettes to combine the two groups. To pull a palette out of a group, drag the tab for the palette to an open area of your screen. You can also move a palette into an existing group (or create a new group) by dragging it on top of any of the tabs found in another palette. To re-order the palettes within a group, just drag one of the tabs to the right or left until the others move aside.

Minimizing A Palette

Any palette can be minimized to only show its tabs by doing one of the following: **1)** double-clicking on any tab in the palette, **2)** double-clicking on the horizontal bar above the tabs, **3)** clicking the horizontal line icon that appears near the upper right corner of each palette. The palette can be restored to its original size by repeating any of the choices listed above, or by clicking on a tab in the palette that is not active.

Closing Palettes

In previous versions of Photoshop, there was no way to close a single palette that was part of a group without first pulling the palette out of the group. In CS3, each palette's tab has its own close symbol (the "X" in the upper right corner), which makes closing individual palettes much easier. You can also close an entire group by clicking on the "X" that's found in the upper right corner of the group.

Show/Hide Palettes

At any time you can press **Tab** to hide all the palettes (plus the Toolbar and Options bar). Pressing **Tab** a second time will bring the palettes back into view. If you'd like to hide the palettes, but keep the Toolbar and Options bar, press **Shift-Tab** instead.

If pressing **Tab** doesn't hide or show your palettes, press **Return** (Mac), or **Enter** (Win) and try again. **Tab** is also used to cycle between fields in a palette or dialog box. Pressing **Return** or **Enter** will have Photoshop accept whichever field might be active and allow the **Tab** key to do its other duty of hiding your palettes.

Now that you know the basics, it's time to get into a completely new way of working with palettes by storing them in a dock.

Palette Docks

A Dock is essentially a container for palettes that is attached to the left or right edge of your screen. That are many advantages to working with docks, but before we get into that, you'll have to learn how to create and populate a dock

Creating & Configuring Docks

To create a dock, drag a palette tab (or the bar above it if you want to use the entire group of palettes) to the left or right edge of your screen. Only release the mouse button when you see a blue vertical bar appear, which is your indication that the palettes are about to be stored in a dock. That will cause the palette to expand, filling the full height of your screen and it will be surrounded by a dark gray border, which designates it as being in a dock.

Populating a Dock

You can place additional palettes into the dock by dragging them to the top or bottom of the docked palette (only release the mouse button when you see a horizontal blue bar appear on the edge of the docked palette). You can also drag palettes into or out of docked palette groups just like you can when they are not docked. You cannot move the dock itself, only the palettes and palette groups that reside within it.

Palettes stored in a Dock.

Re-sizing Palettes in a Dock

Once you have a collection of palettes in a dock, you can resize the individual palettes just as you would if they were not stored in a dock. Changing the width of a docked palette will affect the width of all the palettes in the dock. Just because the dock started out spanning the full height of your screen doesn't mean that you can't drag the bottom edge of the dock to limit its height. Keep in mind that some palettes have a minimum or maximum size, which might limit your choices.

Multiple Docks

You can have more than one dock side by side on the edge of your screen. To add a second dock, drag a palette or group of palettes to the left or right edge of an existing dock and watch for a blue bar to appear on the edge of the dock before releasing the mouse button.

Collapsed Docks

Here's where the fun starts: Once you have populated a dock with palettes, you can collapse all the palettes into icons by clicking on the double arrow icon that is found in the upper right corner of the dock (click the icon a second time to expand the dock back to its original size).

The first time you collapse a dock, the palettes within it will be shown as labeled icons. Once you get used to which icons represent which palettes, you can drag the dark gray edge of the palette, or the gripper bar that appears at the top of the collapsed dock to condense the icon down so that the name becomes hidden. To make the names visible again, just drag the bar in the opposite direction.

Collapsed dock with and without labels.

Palettes that are displayed as icons can be reorganized just like normal palettes. That means you can drag the gray bar at the top of an icon grouping to move the entire icon group, or drag the icon itself to move a single palette.

Working with Collapsed Palettes

When the palettes in a dock have been collapsed into icons, you can only access a single palette at a time without expanding the entire dock. Clicking on any palette icon will expand just that palette. To collapse the palette back into its icon, either click the tab for the palette, click the palette's icon a second time, or click the icon for a different palette to change which palette is open.

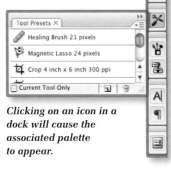

Clicking on an icon in a dock will cause the associated palette to appear.

If you'd like the palettes to automatically collapse when you click outside of them, **Right-click** (Win), or **Control-click** (Mac) on any of the docked palettes and choose **Auto-Collapse Icon Palettes** from the pop-up menu that appears. When that setting is turned on, clicking anywhere outside the palette will cause it to automatically collapse back into its icon. This is a universal setting that applies to all collapsed palettes. I wish I could choose it on a palette by palette basis, but that's just not possible. However if you can get used to the auto-collapsing feature, it can save an awful lot of clicking and that's a good thing, right?

The other thing I wish I could do is to store collapsed palettes below Photoshop's Toolbar. There is always a bunch of unused space in that area that I wish I could utilize more effectively. Maybe they'll let us do that in Photoshop CS4!

Auto-Show Dock

Here's a feature you don't want to miss out on. When you press Tab to hide all the palettes, the docked palettes will become hidden along with all the others, but you can mouse over to the edge of your screen where the dock was configured and a gray bar will appear. Pausing on top of the gray bar (no need to click the mouse button) will cause any docks configured for that side of your screen to appear! Clicking on any other area of your screen will then cause the dock to hide again. That means you can work in full screen mode (which we'll discuss later in this chapter) where your image will fill your screen and then quickly access any docked palette without having them visible all the time. This is an especially elegant improvement to the palette system.

Feeling Nostalgic?

Photoshop CS3 defaults to having your palettes stored in both expanded and collapsed docks. If you'd prefer to work in a way that more closely resembles CS2's environment, remember that you can always pull a palette out of a dock by dragging its tab (or the bar above it for the entire group of palettes) to an open area of your screen. If you drag all of the palettes out of the dock, you'll no longer be using docks, and the palettes will essentially act much like Photoshop CS2's palettes did, but without the use of a Palette Well.

Now that you've met the new Palette Docks, let's move on and explore the changes Adobe made to Photoshop's screen modes.

Revised Screen Modes

For well over a decade you've been able to press **F** to enter full screen mode, or click the associated icons that are found near the bottom of the Toolbar. Well, this time around, Adobe did some tinkering with this feature and it might take some time to adjust to the changes. Let's take a look at what's new in screen modes.

The Icon That Morphed Into a Menu

In previous versions of Photoshop, the screen modes could be accessed by clicking on one of three icons that resided near the bottom of Photoshop's Toolbar. Those three icons have been combined and morphed into a pop-up menu that resides at the bottom of the Toolbar. This happened for two reasons: **1)** Photoshop now offers a single-column Toolbar which just doesn't have room for all those icons (especially when a simple menu could be used), and **2)** a fourth screen mode was added, so even the normal two-column Toolbar would look a little cramped with that many icons. The icon used for the new menu changes depending on which screen mode is currently active. That way you can easily determine which mode you're in. You can click the icon to switch between the modes, or click and hold to access a menu where you can go directly to a specific screen mode. But before we get into the changes they've made to the individual modes, let's look at a few more pertinent issues.

CS2's Toolbar

When you choose a screen mode from the menu (or press **F** to cycle through them), all open documents will change into the chosen screen mode (to do that in CS2 you had to hold Shift when clicking the icon). This change will

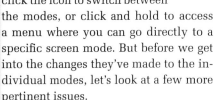

CS3's Toolbar & Full Screen menu.

also persist after creating additional documents or opening existing ones until you reach a time that no documents are open. At that point, any newly opened documents will open into either Standard Screen Mode or the new Maximized Screen mode depending on which one of those two were last in use. This is true, even if the only time you ever entered Maximized Screen Mode was when you typed F multiple times to get to one of the other screen modes. If you'd prefer to use a different mode when opening files, choose from either Standard Screen Mode or Maximized Screen Mode while no documents are open.

Change Surround Color

When you are in any screen mode other than Standard Screen Mode, your image will be surrounded with a solid color (assuming you zoom out enough that the image does not fill the entire screen). In previous versions of Photoshop, you had to know a double-secret trick to change that color (**Shift-click** with the Paintbucket tool on the surrounding color). It's much easier to change the

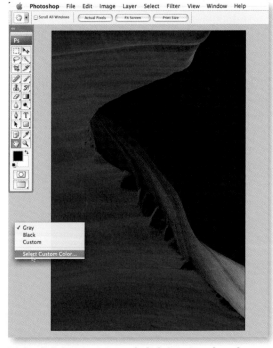

Right-click (Win), or Control-click (Mac) on the color that surrounds the image to choose a different color.

color in CS3. All you have to do is **Right-click** (Win), or **Control-click** (Mac) on the color that surrounds your image (regardless of which tool is active). You'll then be able to choose between **Gray**, **Black** and **Custom** (or instead of using the menu, hold down the **Spacebar** and type **F** to cycle through the preset colors). If you choose **Custom**, Photoshop will use the last custom color you chose (assuming you changed it at some point in the past). If you don't want to use the same custom color, select **Choose Custom Color** from the same menu to access a color picker.

Shift-F Goes Backwards

In previous versions of Photoshop, typing **Shift-F** while in full-screen mode would show or hide the menu bar at the top of your screen. That's no longer the case in CS3. The new setup makes **F** go forward in the list of available screen modes, while **Shift-F** moves you backward in the list.

That means if you prefer to work in Full Screen Mode (where you usually have the menu bar hidden and black surrounding your image), pressing **Shift-F** will send you into Full Screen with Menu Bar mode, which will effectively show the menu bar, but will have the side effect of switching the surround color to gray (which is the default for that mode). To avoid the sudden flash of gray, switch to Full Screen with Menu Bar mode, **Right-click** (Win), or **Control-click** (Mac) on the color that surrounds your image and set it to Black so it matches the surround used in Full Screen Mode. With this new setup, you'll have to type **F** (instead of **Shift-F**) to hide the menu bar again by returning to Full Screen Mode.

Maximized Screen Mode

A new screen mode has been introduced in CS3– Maximized Screen Mode. What makes it unique is that unlike the Full Screen Mode choices, this mode will not allow docked palettes to cover up any part of the image (old-style floating palettes still can). Not only that, it offers scroll bars when your image extends beyond the edge of your monitor and displays the normal document size statistics that usually are visible in the lower left corner of a Standard Screen Mode file.

Using this mode along with docked palettes should help to avoid common problems such as defects in images being obscured by a palette. We've all had this happen, where we missed an important flaw (that needed retouching) because it was hiding behind a palette.

I really like the new Maximized Screen Mode for when I teach hands-on Photoshop classes. Beginners (and Windows users who might be forced to use a Mac during class) often accidentally click on the Mac's desktop, which causes all of Photoshop's palettes to go away (because they have unknowingly just switched to another application). Turning on Maximized Screen Mode before class begins (while no documents are open) can prevent this from happening because the area surrounding the image will no longer be empty, consequently the desktop will not be visible behind it.

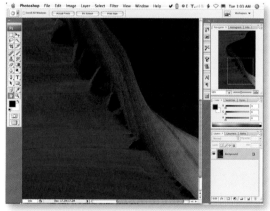

Maximized Screen Mode in action.

Misc. Changes

Now let's explore the less dramatic changes that have happened to Photoshop's user interface.

Single Column Toolbar

When Adobe first released Photoshop, thirteen-inch monitors were the norm and the Toolbar took up a good portion of the vertical space available on-screen. Times have changed since then. Today, I work on a 30" Apple Cinema Display, which features a resolution of 2560x1600 and at that resolution, the Toolbar takes up just over one quarter of the vertical space available on-screen. That leaves a huge amount of unused (and wasted) space in the area below the Toolbar.

To help with this situation, Adobe now offers a single-column Toolbar that uses the space on your monitor more efficiently. If you prefer the old two-column Toolbar, all you have to do is click on the tiny double arrow icon that appears on the top edge of the Toolbar. That will toggle you between the single-column and dual-column Toolbars. After forcing myself to use the single-column Toolbar for a month, I've simply gotten used to it. That doesn't mean I didn't swear at Adobe a few times during the adjustment period though.

Single-Column Toolbar.

Easy Access to Workspaces

Once you get the palettes configured to your liking, I recommend saving the result as a Workspace. To save the position of your palettes so you can easily return to that layout in the future, choose **Save Workspace** from the **Window>Workspace** menu and assign it a name. Workspaces can also include changes you've made to the menus and keyboard shortcuts by using the appropriate commands that are found at the bottom of the Edit menu. A Workspace is not new to CS3, but there is a new way to access them.

Once you've saved a Workspace, you can return to that setup of palettes by choosing the name you assigned to it from the **Window>Workspace** menu or by choosing from the new Workspace pop-up menu that appears in the Options bar that runs across the top of your screen (regardless of which tool is active). You can also save Workspaces from this menu. It's not a huge change, but it does make switching between Workspaces easier.

As you can see, Adobe went for the "extreme makeover" when they decided to update the palette system. As with any radical change there will be both dissenters and supporters feverishly weighing in with their opinions. For me, it was the single-column Toolbar that took me the longest to adjust to. Regardless of whether your first impression is horror or delight, the new furniture is here to stay, so I recommend you approach it with a wide open mind and just run with it. Once you get over the initial discomfort, I predict that you'll be quite surprised at what it can do for you in terms of saving you valuable screen real estate, and boosting your overall efficiency. Before you know it, you'll be whizzing in and out of your palettes and docks like a champion race car driver. No brakes necessary.

The new Workspace menu can be found on the right side of the Options bar that extends across the top of the screen.

Chapter 4
Adjustments

TWO SIGNIFICANT CHANGES WERE MADE in the Adjustments menu: The Curves dialog box received a major update, and the new Black & White converter has taken us out of the dark ages of Photoshop and made it possible to quickly and easily get a great looking grayscale image out of a color original.

Below is an overview of what we'll be covering in this chapter:

- **Curves:** The Curves dialog box got a radical makeover. Not only has it graduated to being one of the most useful tools in Photoshop, it's now possible to tell what's happening to the quality of your image while you're making the adjustment. Control freaks rejoice!
- **Black & White:** If you've ever struggled with color to black & white conversions, you'll love this awesome new adjustment tool which makes the conversion a faster and more intuitive process. In seconds you can get gorgeous, high-quality grayscale images.
- **HDR & 32-Bit:** HDR capability was added in CS2 and now Adobe has expanded the features that are available. This is especially useful for photographers and people who work with video and 3D software.
- **Misc. Changes:** See what smaller changes were made to Levels, Brightness/Contrast, and a new way of applying Variations and Shadow/Highlight adjustments.

Where's My Stuff?

Before we move on to the newest adjustment enhancements, let's look at what's happened to some of the features you might have used in previous versions of Photoshop:

- **Curves–Flip Gradients Icon:** If you're used to clicking on the small double triangle icon that appears in the middle of the bottom gradient (to switch between working with light and ink), you'll now have to click on the Curve Display Options icon at the bottom of the dialog box and toggle between the Light and Pigment/Ink settings.

- **Curves–Small/Large Curve Icon:** Photoshop CS2 offered an icon that allowed you to switch between a small and large Curves display. Photoshop CS3 only offers the larger version of the Curves dialog box.

- **Curves–Load & Save Buttons:** The Load & Save buttons have been replaced by the new Preset menu at the top of the Curves dialog box. To save the current curve as a preset, click the icon that appears to the right of the Preset menu, choose **Save Preset** and then assign it a name. To access the preset in the future, just choose its name from the Presets pop-up menu at the top of the dialog box. You can also choose Load Preset from the same icon menu to load curves that you've saved from previous versions of Photoshop. If you'd like older presets to appear in the Presets menu in CS3, move the files to the following directory on your hard drive:
  Mac: **Users*Current User*\\Library\\ Application Support\\Adobe\\ Adobe Photoshop CS3\\Presets\\Curves**
  Win XP: **C:\\Documents and Settings\\ *Current User*\\Application Data\\Adobe\\Adobe Photoshop CS3\\Presets\\Curves**
  Win Vista: **C:\\Users*Current User*\\AppData\\ Roaming\\Adobe\\Adobe Photoshop CS3\\ Presets\\Curves**
- **Curves–Simplicity:** If the new Curves dialog box looks cluttered with features you're not used to, click the Curve Display Options icon and turn off all the checkboxes that appear. This should get you as close to the way things used to work as possible in the new Curves dialog box.
- **Brightness/Contrast–Same Results:** Adobe has improved how the Brightness/Contrast adjustment affects images (it's a big improvement). To make it work like it did in previous versions of Photoshop, turn on the Use Legacy checkbox within the Brightness/Contrast dialog box.

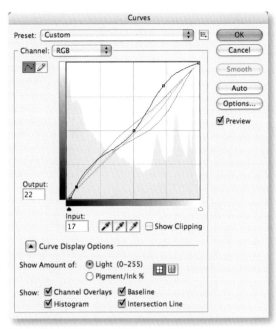

Photoshop CS3's updated Curves dialog box.

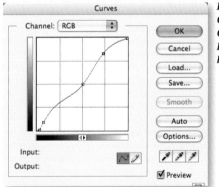

Photoshop CS2's Curves Dialog box.

Curves

The Curves dialog box has remained nearly untouched for years, so the major surgery it got in CS3 caused quite a stir. Sometimes changes to favorite features are unnerving, but in this case I think you'll love the new goodies in Curves. The list of changes is large and includes what most users have been asking for. In the past, I used Levels for grayscale images and simple adjustments because it offered a few features that

NOTE

Learning Curves
This book is all about getting you up to speed on the new features in CS3. Since Curves has been in Photoshop since version 1.0 (back in 1990), we'll spend a limited amount of time learning about Curves in this book. For the most in-depth information about Curves, check out the Understanding Curves chapter in my book *Photoshop CS3 Studio Techniques* (Adobe Press).

were not found in Curves (like a histogram for instance). But since I've been working in CS3, I haven't touched Levels because Curves can do everything that's available in Levels and a whole lot more.

If you're not already comfortable with Curves (it's by no means a new feature since it's been in Photoshop for over 15 years), don't worry. I'll give you an overview of how to use it before we plunge into the changes that were made in CS3. If you're already comfortable using Curves, you might want to skip the next section and get right into the new stuff starting on page 67.

Introducing Curves

I consider Curves to be the most powerful and versatile adjustment in all of Photoshop. Many of those other adjustments (like Brightness/Contrast, Levels, and Color Balance) are actually using Curves behind the scenes while trying to present you with a more user-friendly interface. The problem with that is that anytime Adobe tries to simplify the interface (by turning it into a dialog box with a few sliders, like Levels), they always end up with a tool that has nowhere near the versatility of the real thing. Knowing how to

use Curves can help raise the quality of your images to a level that is far beyond what the simpler adjustments can do.

Curves is on the list of features that many people are afraid of (Channels, the Pen tool and Displacement Maps come to mind). Curves is on the list because it is not easy to learn on your own and it's easy to screw up your image if you don't know what you're doing. Don't let that hold you back. I'll walk you through the basics so you can get started using them right away with confidence that you won't hurt your images. So if you've been taking the easy way out with those inferior adjustment tools, there has never been a better time to leave them behind and throw yourself whole-heartedly into Curves.

The Basics

When you open the Curves dialog box, you'll be presented with a grid that contains a diagonal line. The straight line indicates that no adjustment has been made yet (it would be curved if an adjustment were being applied). The gradient at the bottom

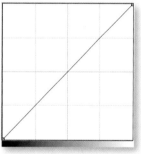

The curve always starts as a diagonal line.

of the grid represents all the brightness levels in your image, and the diagonal line indicates how much light or ink would be needed to create the shades in the gradient.

Just look at the graph above where Photoshop is using light to create the image (I'll show you how to switch from light to ink in a moment). The line is all the way at the bottom above black to indicate that no light is needed to produce black. The line is all the way to the top above white to indicate that you'd need to use as much light as possible to create white. If you look at the position of the line above any of the shades in the gradient, you'll see exactly how much light would be needed to create them.

You can switch between working with light and ink by clicking on the Curve Display Options icon at the bottom of the Curves dialog box and then switching between the Light and Pigment/Ink settings. All that does is switch the orientation of the gradient, which causes the gradient to reflect what you'd get if you used the amount of ink represented by the diagonal line (no ink to create white and 100% ink to create black; it's the exact opposite of how light works). Using light or ink is a personal choice and does not necessarily reflect how you plan to reproduce your image. I find most photographers are more comfortable thinking about light, while graphic designers and prepress professionals prefer thinking about ink. I'm going to use the Light setting throughout this explanation of Curves because that's the setting I personally prefer.

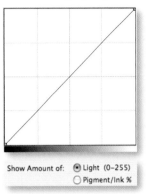

The Light setting produces black by using no light.

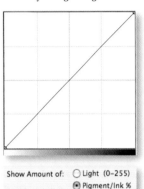

The Ink setting produces black by using 100% ink.

Height Determines Brightness

If you click within your image while the Curves dialog box is open, you will see a circle appear on the diagonal line which will indicate how much light is being used to create that area in your image. You can also look at the part of the horizontal gradient directly below the circle to see how bright the area is that you are clicking on. If you want to adjust the brightness of an area, hold **Command** (Mac), or **Ctrl** (Win) and click within your image to add a point to the curve. After adding a point, you can move the point vertically to change how much light is used in that area of your image. If you move it up, you'll add light to an area and therefore brighten it. If you move the point down, you'll decrease the amount of light in the area and therefore darken it.

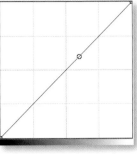

The circle is the result of clicking within the image.

When adjusting the brightness, try to (at first) just concentrate on the area that you clicked on and largely ignore what's happening to the rest of the image until the area you targeted becomes as bright as you desire. Then notice the rest of the image. Moving a point up or down will affect the majority of the curve and therefore change the brightness of the majority of your image, so it's not unlikely that other areas could change in undesirable ways. To correct for that you can **Command-click** (Mac), or **Ctrl-click** (Win) on those areas—which adds points—and use those new points to move the curve up or down to control the brightness of those areas.

Here's an example of how I used Curves to darken part of an image: I started by **Command-clicking** (Mac), or **Ctrl-clicking** (Win) on the bright area near the top of the image. I then moved the point that was added to the curve down until I liked the brightness of that area. But, after making that simple adjustment, I noticed that the darker areas were too dark. To fix that problem, I **Command-clicked** (Mac), or **Ctrl-clicked** (Win) on a dark area and moved the curve up to add light and brighten the area.

> **NOTE**
>
> **CMYK is Different**
> *Clicking on your image while in CMYK mode will not produce a circle in the Curves dialog box, and Command or Ctrl-clicking on the image will not create a point on the curve. You'll instead need to try to find the brightness level you're clicking on from the gradient at the bottom of the Curves dialog box and then look at the area of the curve that appears directly above that shade to determine where to manually add a point.*

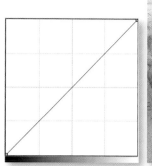

Original image before adjustment.

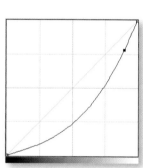

This adjustment precisely adjusts the amount of light in the brighter area of this image.

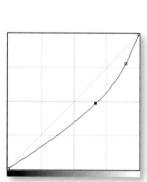

Adding a second point for the darker areas allowed for independent control of that area.

If you want to brighten or darken an isolated area, you may need to add additional points to the curve and adjust their locations to keep the majority of the curve in its original position while only allowing a small area of the curve to move up or down.

On the left edge of the Curves grid is a vertical gradient that shows you how bright an area will become if you move a point to a particular height. For instance, if you move a point all the way to the bottom you'll make an area black, while moving it all the way to the top will produce white, etc. I usually ignore this gradient and simply watch the image to see when it becomes the desired brightness.

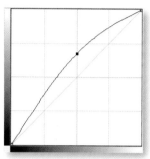

The gradient to the left of the curve shows you how bright you'll make an area if you move the curve to any height.

Angle Determines Contrast & Detail

The angle of the curve will determine how much contrast you end up with in an area. Making the curve steeper (more toward a vertical line) will produce a greater difference between light and dark therefore increasing contrast and exaggerating detail. Making the curve flatter (more toward a horizontal line) will make the brightness levels in an area more similar, which will decrease contrast and make it more difficult to see detail.

To change the contrast of an area, start by clicking and dragging across the area while watching the circle move across the curve. Note the area of the curve that the circle runs across and then add a point on each end of that area. Once you've done that, you have three choices on how to make the curve steeper or flatter. When increasing contrast:

Two points added.

1) Move the upper dot further up to brighten the brightest part of the area you dragged across while leaving the darkest area unchanged.

2) Move the lower dot further down to darken the darkest area while keeping the bright area unchanged.

3) Move the upper dot up and the lower dot down to brighten the bright park and darken the dark part.

When decreasing contrast, you have the following three choices:

1) Move the upper point down to make the bright areas more similar to the dark ones (while not changing the brightness of the dark areas).

2) Move the lower point up to make the dark areas more similar to the bright ones (while not changing the brightness of the bright areas).

3) Move the upper point down and the lower point up to both darken the bright areas and brighten the dark areas.

Here's an example of adding contrast to an image: I started by dragging across the flat area on the left of the image to see where the circle ran in the Curves dialog box. I then added a point on each side of that area and moved one point up and the other one down (option 3 from the list for adding contrast) to boost the contrast and make more detail pop out.

Original image before adjustment.

After doing that, I noticed the triangular area to the right became more colorful and I wanted it to remain unchanged. I clicked and dragged across that area, added two points in the general proximity of that area and adjusted them until the curve went back to its original position, which brought that area back to normal.

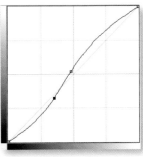

Steepening the curve to increase contrast.

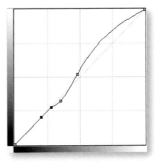

Preventing changes to the darker portion of the image.

Two Things to Look Out For

After you've adjusted the brightness or contrast of an area, look over the curve and scan for potential problems. There are two common situations that will cause your image to look terrible:

Flat Equals No Detail When adjusting the brightness or contrast of an image, you might inadvertently cause part of the curve to become perfectly flat. That will make the part of your image that used to have detail to appear as a solid color with zero detail. This is most common when the curve ends up either bottoming out or topping out. When that happens, click in the middle of the flat part of the curve to add a point, then drag the newly added point toward the point that is farthest away

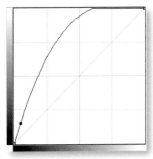
This point was added to brighten the shadows, but that caused the highlights to become blown out (no detail) as indicated by the flat area of the curve.

(of the two dots that are adjacent to the one you just added). Then move the point around in a little circle while you watch the overall shape of the curve. The idea is to find the position that prevents the flat spot while producing a smooth looking curve.

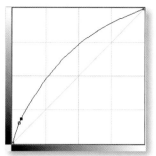

The second point was added to prevent the curve from "topping out."

Avoid Downhill At All Costs After adjusting an image, mentally trace the resulting curve starting from the lower left corner and moving toward the right. Ideally, the curve should always go "uphill" as you move toward the right. If any part of the curve goes downhill instead of up, you're going to have problems on your hands. A downhill curve will cause part of the image to be inverted (dark areas becoming bright while formerly bright areas become dark). When this happens, try to be less aggressive with the adjustment you are performing to see if it will prevent the downhill issue. I guarantee you that every time you let the curve go downhill you will not like the look of the image.

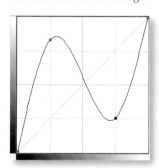 

The curve shown above was applied to the original image to produce the result shown in the lower right.

Channels for Color Shifts

Behind the scenes, a color image is made out of three or four colors which reflect the color mode of the image (Red, Green & Blue or Cyan, Magenta, Yellow & Black). The **Channels** pop-up menu near the top of the Curves dialog box will determine how many of these colors will be affected by your adjustment. Leaving the menu at its default setting will adjust all of the colors an equal amount, which will change the brightness of the image without affecting its color. Choosing one of the colors from the **Channels** pop-up menu will allow you to control exactly how much of that particular color is used within your image.

Moving the Red curve up will cause the image to become brighter (because you're using more light) and more reddish (because you're increasing the amount of red light used to make up the image). Moving the **Red** curve down will cause the image to become darker and less red. If the image didn't

Original image before adjustment.

look overly red to begin with, this will usually cause the image to shift toward cyan since cyan ink absorbs red light and is considered the opposite of red—just as green light is absorbed by magenta ink and blue light is absorbed by yellow ink. If you have trouble remembering which color of ink absorbs each color of light, either

> **NOTE**
>
> **Color Curves**
> *For more in-depth information on how to adjust the individual color curves, check out the Understanding Curves and Color Manipulation chapters in my book **Photoshop CS3 Studio Techniques** (published by Adobe Press).*

> **NOTE**
>
> **Composite Curve**
> *The curve you're presented with when the Channels pop-up menu is set to RGB is known as the composite curve. Any changes you make to this curve are applied as if it was making identical changes to each of the individual color curves, but the change will only appear on the composite curve.*

Moving the Red curve up gives you more red.

Moving the Red curve down uses less red, as if you were using cyan ink to absorb the red.

Moving the Green curve up gives you more green.

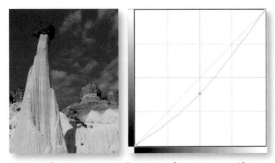

Moving the Green curve down uses less green, as if you were using magenta ink to absorb the green.

Moving the Blue curve up makes the image more blue.

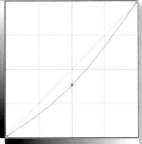

Moving the Blue curve down uses less blue, as if you were using yellow ink to absorb the blue.

Use the Info palette to remind you which color of ink is the opposite of each color of light.

move each color curve wildly to see how your image shifts, or open the Info palette by choosing **Window>Info**. This handy palette will show the colors of light on the left side and the colors of ink that absorb them on the right.

Adjusting the individual color channels can be useful when an image has a color cast or when you'd like the image to have a warmer or cooler feeling.

Now that you have an idea of how to think about Curves, let's start to explore the features that were added in Photoshop CS3. To access most of these features, you'll have to click on the Curve Display Options icon at the bottom of the Curves dialog box.

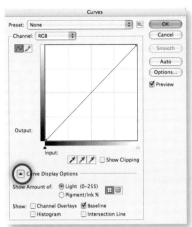

Click the expansion triangle icon to the left of Curve Display Options to expand the dialog box.

Histogram

If you could run your image through an X-ray machine the result would most certainly end up looking like a histogram. And there's nothing better than a histogram to tell you if your image has any problems with color or tone. CS3 has integrated this wonderful diagnostic tool right into the Curves interface so you can make intelligent decisions while you're making an adjustment.

Turning on the Histogram checkbox will cause a bar chart to be overlaid on the curve. The chart indicates how prevalent each of the brightness levels are that are found in the horizontal bar at the bottom of the Curves grid. One bar on the chart will always extend all the way to the top of the Curves grid to indicate which shade is the most prevalent, while the other bars show how the less prevalent shades compare to the one that is most prevalent. If no bar is shown above a particular brightness level, then that shade is nowhere to be found in the image. There are three main concepts I use when analyzing the Histogram found in the Curves dialog box:

> **NOTE**

Histogram Palette
The Histogram found in the Curves dialog box will always indicate the brightness levels that were present before the Curves adjustment was applied. If you'd like to see a histogram that shows the results of your adjustment, then open the Histogram palette by choosing **Window>Histogram**.

Analyze Brightness Range

When looking at a Histogram, the width will be an indication of the brightness range present in an image. If the histogram does not cover the full width of the Curves grid, the image you are adjusting does not contain the full brightness range from black to white. A gap on the left end of the histogram indicates that the darkest area of the image is not very dark and contains no blacks. A gap on the right side of the histogram indicates that the brightest area of the image is not close to being white. Many images will look their best if they contain the full brightness range. This can be accomplished by either performing color correction—using the eyedroppers in Curves, or adjusting the new Black and White point sliders—which we'll discuss later in this chapter.

This histogram indicates that the image does not contain any overly bright or dark information.

This histogram indicates that the image does not contain any overly dark information.

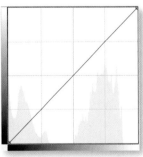

This histogram indicates that the image does not contain any overly bright information.

If the histogram for an unadjusted image extends all the way across the Curves grid, you should inspect the first and last bar on the chart. If either one of those bars are tall, it indicates that your image might be lacking shadow or high-light detail because there is a large area of either solid black

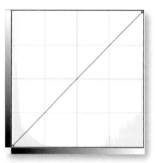

The spike on the first bar of this histogram indicates the image contains a large area of solid black, while the spike on the right indicates a large area of solid white.

(indicated by a spike on the left end of the histogram) or solid white (indicated by a spike on the right). We'll talk more about lost highlight and shadow detail (often known as clipping) when we talk about the new Clipping Display feature later in this chapter.

Check for Saturation Clipping

The histogram can also be useful when viewing the individual color curves (via the **Channels** pop-up menu near the top of the Curves dialog box). If a tall spike is visible on either end of the histogram for the individual color channels, areas of your image that contain saturated colors might be losing detail. This is often caused by an over adjustment of the Saturation slider in the Hue/Saturation dialog box. There's no way to bring back the lost detail while in the Curves dialog box (you'd have to undo the Hue/Saturation adjustment and use a lower setting), but at least you can tell when it's happening.

Add Contrast Without Compromise

Anytime you increase contrast in one brightness range (by making the curve steeper), you'll end up decreasing it in another (by making it flatter). Flattening out the curve will make it more difficult to see detail, which can be problematic in many images. The histogram can help you cheat in some cases by allowing you to sacrifice detail in brightness ranges that are not very prevalent in the image, so that you can get away with boosting the contrast in the rest of the image.

Left: Original image before the adjustment.
Right: Result of applying the adjustment shown below.

When you notice a histogram that contains a low flat area, try adding a dot on both ends of that area on the curve above to mark where the flat part starts and stops. Then move the upper dot down and the lower dot up until they are at approximately the same height to flatten the curve above the flat part of the histogram. This will increase the contrast in the rest of the image (by making the rest of the curve steeper) while sacrificing it in the flat area. In these situations think of it as being able to have your cake (contrast in this case) and eat it too (by not messing up your image). It will only work on those special images that feature a low flat area, so don't expect it to work on most images.

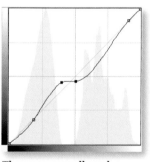

The curve was allowed to become flat in the area directly above the part of the histogram that does not have any tall bars visible.

Intersection Line

Turning on the Intersection Line checkbox will cause a light gray horizontal and vertical line to extend from your cursor when moving a point on the curve. This is to help you see how the point relates to the horizontal and vertical gradients that appear in the Curves dialog box. The horizontal gradient indicates which brightness level you're adjusting in your image, while the vertical gradient indicates how the brightness level will change as the result of your adjustment. These intersection lines can also be useful when trying to line up a point with a particular area of the histogram (like what we discussed above about sneaky contrast adjustments).

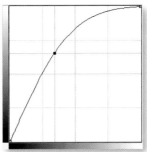

Turning on the Intersection Line feature will cause a horizontal and vertical line to extend from the point you are currently moving.

I personally find the intersection line makes the Curves dialog box look too cluttered and complex, so I rarely turn it on.

Curves As A Levels Replacement?

In previous versions of Photoshop, I'd often choose Levels over Curves when adjusting gray-scale images or when working on masks. The reason for this was three-fold:

1) Levels felt simpler with only five sliders to deal with and most of the time only three of them were necessary.
2) Levels offered a histogram that was not available in Curves and the histogram was useful in determining if an image contained any black or white.
3) Levels offered a Clipping Display that indicated exactly which areas in an image were becoming solid black or white.

All those features are now available in Photoshop CS3's updated Curves dialog box, which makes Levels less essential. In fact, I've completely stopped using Levels in CS3, and I'm now campaigning for people to give up Levels altogether, and go for Curves instead. If you take some time now to really understand Curves and learn to use it with confidence, I promise you will never regret saying goodbye to Levels. But enough campaigning for now, let's continue with Black/White Point sliders.

Black/White Point Sliders

The two sliders found near the lower right and lower left corners of the Curves grid are known as the Black and White Point sliders. They replicate the upper left and right sliders that are found in the Levels dialog box.

> **NOTE**
>
> **Black/White Points**
> *You can replicate the functionality of the new Black and White Point sliders in previous versions of Photoshop by simply moving the lower left point on the curve toward the right (for the black point) and the upper right point toward the left (for the white point). In fact, that's exactly what these new sliders do. It's just an attempt to get people who are used to Levels to be more comfortable working in Curves.*

When you move the black slider toward the right, you'll force the shade it points to in the gradient to black along with all the shades that are found to the left of the slider. Moving the white slider toward the left will force the shade it points at to white along with all the shades found to the right of the slider. Here's an example of when you might use them:

If you have an image that does not contain the full brightness range (no blacks or whites as indicated by a histogram that does not extend all the way across the Curves grid), consider using the new Black and White Point sliders to adjust the image. Start by dragging the black triangle that appears in the lower left corner of the Curves grid toward the right until it touches the left edge of the histogram. That will cause the darkest area of the image to become black. Next, move the white slider that appears in the lower right corner of the Curves grid toward the left until it touches the right edge of the histogram. That will cause the brightest area of the image to become white.

Once you've done that with both sliders, you should end up with an image that contains the full brightness range available. With that accomplished, you can start to adjust the overall brightness and contrast of the image by manipulating the rest of the curve.

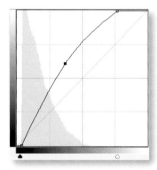

The Black & White Point sliders were adjusted to produce the full brightness range in this image. An additional point was added and moved up to brighten the image overall.

I mainly use the Black and White Point sliders on grayscale images because performing color correction on a color image will usually cause it to contain the full brightness range available, which makes these sliders less than essential on color images. In fact, the eyedroppers in the Curves dialog box (which are used for color correction) use the Black and White Point sliders to do their work. They simply do it on the individual color channels instead of the main curve.

Clipping Display

A clipping display can show you which areas of your image are becoming solid black or solid white as the result of your adjustment. It's an especially useful little feature that tells you if you're pushing your adjustment too far. There are three ways to get a clipping display in the updated Curves dialog box:

1) Hold **Option** (Mac), or **Alt** (Win) when moving the Black Point slider to see which areas are becoming solid black.

2) Hold **Option** (Mac), or **Alt** (Win) when moving the White Point slider to see which areas are becoming solid white.

3) Turn on the Clipping Display checkbox near the bottom of the Curves dialog box and then press **Control-Tab** to cycle between the black and white clipping displays (or click on the Black and White eyedropper icons in the Curves dialog box).

When using the clipping display, areas that appear in color contain partial detail (also known as saturation clipping) while areas that appear as black (when viewing the black clipping display) or white (when viewing the white clipping display) contain no detail at all.

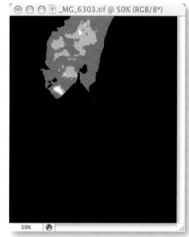

The clipping display showing a small area of solid white along with some saturation clipping as indicated by the white and blue areas.

I prefer my images to contain a small area of solid black and solid white to insure that I'm using the full contrast range available. There are a few exceptions to this rule such as images that contain fog or mist, which might lose their natural-looking quality when adjusted to contain the full brightness range.

I find that light sources and reflections of light sources on very shiny surfaces (like glass, water or polished metal) look best when they are solid white.

Baseline

Turning on the Baseline checkbox will cause Photoshop to overlay a light gray diagonal line over the Curves grid. This line indicates where the curve was positioned before any changes were made and is useful in determining exactly how a curve will af-

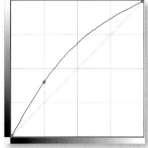

The Baseline represents the position the curve was in before the adjustment.

fect an image. When working with the Light setting, moving the curve above the baseline will brighten the image, while moving it below the line will darken the image (the opposite is true when using the Pigment/Ink setting). When working on the individual color curves (via the **Channels** pop-up menu near the top of the Curves dialog box), moving the curve above the baseline will cause the color of the image to shift toward the color indicated in the pop-up menu, while moving the curve below the baseline will move the overall color of the image away from that color and toward its opposite color (we talked about the concept of opposite colors earlier in this chapter).

I always have the Baseline visible because I find it much easier to analyze how a curve is affecting an image if I can compare it to the original, unadjusted image (as represented by the baseline).

Channel Overlays

When you adjust the individual color channels in Curves (via the **Channels** pop-up menu near the top of the dialog box), you'll cause the overall color in an image to become warmer or cooler. In previous versions of Photoshop, you had to manually switch

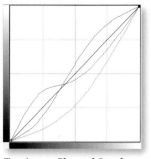

Turning on Channel Overlays will display the color curves overlaid on the main curve.

between the color curves to see if any color shifts were being applied to the image. But now you can simply turn on the Channel Overlays checkbox, which will cause all of the color curves to be overlaid on top of each other making it easy for you to see if color shifts are being made. You'll still have to switch to the individual color curves to make adjustments though.

This overlay can be useful when you want to determine what type of color shift a particular Curves adjustment is making. If one of the color curves ends up above the baseline (the gray diagonal line that appears after turning on the Baseline checkbox), then the image will appear brighter (since more light is being used) and will shift toward the color of the curve. If a color curve appears below the baseline, the image will appear darker (since less light is being used) and will shift toward the opposite of the color of the curve. Red light is absorbed by cyan ink (they are opposites), just as green light is absorbed by magenta ink and blue light is absorbed by yellow ink.

Presets

If you find yourself applying the same curve to many images, you might want to consider saving the curve as a preset. After creating the curve you desire (but before clicking the OK button), click the icon that appears just to the right of the **Presets** pop-up menu at the top of the Curves dialog box and choose **Save Preset** from the menu that appears. Saving the preset into the default location will cause it to appear in the Presets pop-up menu at the top of the Curves dialog box, making it easy to quickly apply the same adjustment to future images. If you don't use the default location, you'll have to click on the icon that appears to the right of the **Presets** pop-up menu and choose **Load Preset** to be able to access the preset.

If you plan to simply apply the same curve to two or three images, there is no need to save a preset. Instead, use one of the following techniques:

1) Use a Curves Adjustment Layer to adjust the first image and after clicking OK, drag the Adjustment Layer from the Layers palette and release your mouse button while it is on top of another open document. This drops a copy of the Adjustment Layer in the other document.

2) Apply a curve by choosing **Image>Adjustments>Curves** and then after clicking OK, switch to another document and hold **Option** (Mac), or **Alt** (Win) while choosing **Image>Adjustments>Curves**, which will get Curves to remember the last settings you applied.

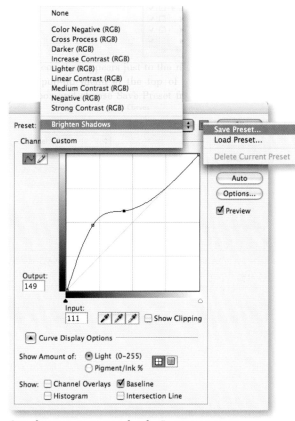

Saved presets appear under the Preset pop-up menu.

Adobe really listened to users when they revamped Curves for CS3. They implemented 99% of the suggestions I made for Curves and I'm happy to say that I have little to complain about. Now, let's move on and explore the other changes Adobe made to the adjustments available in Photoshop.

Black & White

In previous versions of Photoshop, the most common method for converting a color image to black & white was to use the Channel Mixer. It was a clunky, counter-intuitive process that forced you to think like Photoshop instead of allowing your brain and eyes to naturally digest what was being done to your image. The new Black & White converter is a truly wonderful tool that makes the conversion process much more intuitive and user friendly. Because it's so easy to use, it's got an instant gratification aspect to it that makes it especially fun to play with.

Creating a Good Mix

When you choose **Image>Adjustments>Black & White**, all the color will be taken out of your image and you'll be presented with a dialog box that has six primary sliders. You can control the brightness of different areas in your image by dragging the appropriate slider (for instance, the **Reds** slider brightens or darkens areas that used to be red in the image). The only problem with this approach is that you can't see what color different areas used to be without toggling the Preview checkbox.

The new Black & White adjustment.

> ## NOTE
>
> ### P for Preview
> In Photoshop CS3, you can press **P** to toggle the Preview checkbox in most dialog boxes.

You can also click and drag within the main image window to have Photoshop try to figure out the proper slider to affect that area. When working this way, click on the image and (while you're still holding down) simply drag to the left to darken the area, or drag to the right to brighten

it. You'll see the corresponding slider magically move in the Black & White dialog box. I absolutely love working this way, but find that Photoshop doesn't always choose the best slider to isolate the area on which I'm clicking. If you find that it's having trouble isolating an area, toggle the Preview checkbox off and

Original color image.

then back on again and try the sliders in an area similar in color to the area you want to affect. You might find that one chosen manually in this fashion works better than the one that Photoshop automatically selects.

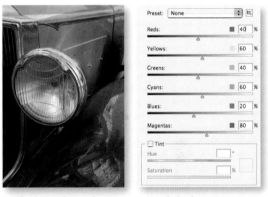

A Black & White adjustment using default settings.

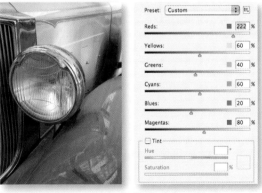

Photoshop chose to move the Reds slider when I dragged across both the fender and the body and was not able to isolate the two colors.

I experimented and found that the Yellows slider would affect the body a lot more than the fender. By adjusting both, I was able to get the results I desired.

Turning on the Tint checkbox will tint your newly created black & white image.

In this example, dragging on either the body of the car or the fender area caused Photoshop to move the **Reds** slider which caused both areas to change in almost equal amounts. By experimenting, I found that the **Yellows** slider did a much better job of isolating the body of the vehicle, so I used the **Yellows** slider to brighten the body and the **Reds** slider to darken the fender of the car.

Watch Out For Clipping

Each of the adjustment sliders in the Black & White dialog box has a very wide range available, which means that it's very easy to end up with solid black or white areas in your image (also known as clipping). If you're concerned about losing detail in the highlight or shadow areas of your image, consider opening the Info palette (by choosing **Window>Info**) and passing over the brightest and darkest areas of the image. If the right side of the RGB readout in the Info palette ever hits zero, you'll know that the area under your mouse is solid black and if it hits 255, then the area is white. I find that turning on the Tint checkbox (which we'll discuss next) can make it easy to tell if you're losing highlight detail. That's because the white areas will contrast with the areas that are being tinted, thus making them easier to see.

> **NOTE**
>
> **Resetting A Slider**
> If you'd like to get one of the color sliders in the Black & White dialog box back to its default position, hold **Option** (Mac), or **Alt** (Win) and click on the color swatch associated with the slider.

Adding a Color Tint

Photographers often add a very subtle hint of color to their black and white conversions to make them feel slightly warm or cool. You can do this to your black & white conversions by turning on the Tint checkbox in the Black & White dialog box. The Hue slider will determine the color used and the Saturation slider will determine the amount of color used.

You can also specify the color by clicking on the color swatch that appears to the right of the Hue and Saturation sliders. If there are particular colors that you prefer to use, consider either saving them as part of a preset (mentioned below), or save the colors into the Swatches palette so you can easily access them in the future. When you want to apply one of the colors, click on the color swatch to the right of the Hue and Saturation sliders to access the color picker and then click on one of the colors in the Swatches palette while the picker is still open.

> **NOTE**
>
> **Compatibility**
> The Black & White adjustment was not available in previous versions of Photoshop, which means that attempting to open an image that has a Black & White Adjustment Layer will cause an error message when using older versions of Photoshop. You'll have to merge or flatten the layers before opening the image in an older version of Photoshop.

Working with Presets

I find that there are certain starting points I prefer when working on different types of images. For landscapes, I might want to make the blue darker to get a nice rich looking sky, while lightening the yellows to get good looking grass and trees (these areas typically contain more yellow than green). For portraits, I might prefer to have lighter yellows, reds and magentas to keep the skin on the pale side while darkening the greens, cyans and blues to contrast them with the skin. You'll have to experiment to figure out what works best for your particular situation. Once you've come up with some good starting points for different types of images, you can save them as presets by clicking on the icon that appears to the left of the OK button and choosing Save Preset. If you assign it a name and save it in the default location, you'll be able to quickly access it in the future by choosing its name from the Preset pop-up menu at the top of the Black & White dialog box.

Tips & Tricks for B&W Conversions

Below are a selection of tips and insights that I think you'll find useful when making black & white conversions:

True Grayscale: Applying a Black & White adjustment does not automatically convert your image to grayscale mode. RGB images take up three times as much space in memory and on your hard drive, so if you want to end up with the most efficient file size, choose **Image>Mode>Grayscale** after converting your image to black & white.

RGB Only: The Black & White adjustment does not work on CMYK or Lab mode images. Choose **Image>Mode>RGB** if you find that the Black & White menu item is not available.

Muted or Low Contrast Originals: If your original image contains mostly muted colors or does not have much contrast, try **Image>Adjustments>Auto Levels** before applying a Black & White adjustment. That should help to produce better separation between the colors in your image.

Auto for Actions: Click on the Auto button in the Black & White dialog box to have Photoshop analyze your image and move the sliders to add contrast. Don't expect this to give you the best results though. It's simply better than the default settings and might be useful if you need to quickly convert dozens of images using an action. When recording the action, just click the Auto button and don't mess with any of the color sliders (otherwise it will record the position of all the sliders instead of the Auto button).

Maximum RGB: You can have Photoshop use the highest value of the red, green and blue numbers that make up each pixel in an image (essentially grabbing the brightest pixel from each of the channels that make up the image). That means Photoshop would analyze an area that contains 100R 200G 50B, and choose the 200 value to use for all three colors (since balanced RGB is needed to produce a shade of gray). For the maximum RGB value, set all the color sliders to +100.

Minimum RGB: Another alternative method of converting to black & white is to use the lowest RGB number for each pixel. To get an image with the minimum RGB values, set all the color sliders to zero.

Straight Red, Green or Blue: You can perform a direct conversion of one of the RGB color channels in your image to a black and white image by doing the following: for the Red channel, set the Red, Yellow and Magenta sliders to 100% and all the others to zero. For the Green channel, set the Green, Yellow and Cyan sliders to 100% and the others to zero. For the Blue channel, set the Blue, Cyan and Yellow sliders to 100% and all the others to zero.

Keyboard Shortcuts: If you're a keyboard shortcut junkie, type **Shift-Option-Command-B** (Mac), or **Shift-Alt-Ctrl-B** (Win) to access the Black & White adjustment dialog box. If you prefer to use Adjustment Layers, consider assigning its keyboard shortcut (via the **Edit>Keyboard Shortcuts** menu) to the **Layer>Adjustment Layers>Black & White** command so that it will produce an Adjustment Layer.

HDR & 32-Bit

The concept of High Dynamic Range images was introduced in Photoshop CS2 (combine multiple exposures into a single file that contains a wider dynamic range than any of the individual shots used to create it). For this version of Photoshop most of the changes are geared toward folks who use this feature for video and 3D. This book's primary audience is made up of graphic designers and photographers, so I'll share the one thing I think would be of use to that group and then give a brief overview of the other changes that have been made.

> **(NOTE)**
>
> **Learning HDR**
> *For complete coverage on what's necessary to shoot, merge and adjust HDR images, check out the High Dynamic Range Imaging chapter in my book **Photoshop CS2: Up to Speed** (published by Peachpit Press).*

Merge to HDR

The changes Adobe made to the Merge to HDR dialog box (accessed via the **Tools>Photoshop** menu in Bridge, or the **File>Automate** menu in Photoshop) appear to be minor at first glance, but they can have a significant impact on the quality of your images.

Improved Auto-Alignment: Photoshop CS2 offered a feature designed to compensate for misregistration between images. The problem was that it was only available in Photoshop—most people preferred to merge their images using Bridge—and it did a really lousy job of aligning the images. In Photoshop CS3, Adobe has come up with a completely new way to align images and the results are simply amazing. I'd almost go as far as saying that you'd have a chance at creating an acceptable HDR image shooting handheld! There isn't anything extra you have to do to use this new technology. Simply turn on the Attempt to Automatically Align Source Images checkbox if merging your images from Photoshop (it's done automatically in Bridge).

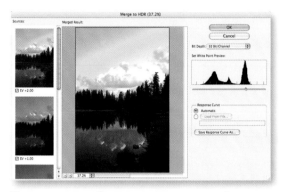

You can now save the camera response curve from within the Merge to HDR dialog box.

Advanced Features

All the other changes they've made to the HDR and 32-bit features are ones that I don't think too many photographers or graphic designers will use so for you deep-tech folks, I will just summarize them here.

Color Picker: The color picker used with 32-bit images now displays the current color with seven different intensity levels and can display the color relative to the active document's exposure setting.

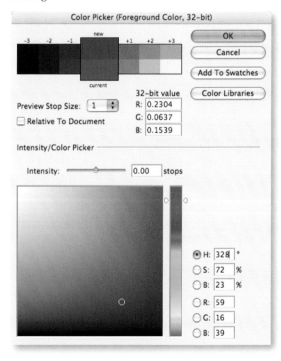

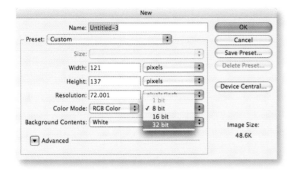

New 32-bit Documents: You can now create 32-bit documents from scratch by setting the **Bit Depth** pop-up menu (which is the unlabeled pop-up menu found to the right of the **Color Mode** pop-up menu) to **32 bit** in the **File>New** dialog box.

Stored Response Curve: Merge to HDR now stores a response curve in Photoshop's preferences for each camera it encounters. It updates this information to improve accuracy each time you merge images shot on the same camera. If you need to retain the same results for future use (instead of using a response curve that might have been updated since the last time you merged a particular set of images into an HDR image), click the Save Response Curve button in the Merge to HDR dialog box. That will save the response curve that was created from the current set of photos you are merging. Then you can load that curve at a later date if you want to have Photoshop ignore the one that is saved in your preferences.

Image Menu Commands: More commands are available in the **Image** menu including Duplicate, Image Size, Canvas Size, Pixel Aspect Ratio, Rotate Canvas, Crop, and Trim. You can also now apply the Calculations and Apply Image commands. The following adjustments have also been enabled for 32-bit images: Hue/Saturation, Desaturate, Levels, Auto Levels, Auto Contrast, Auto Color, Photo Filter.

Filters Menu Commands: A whole bunch of filters have become available in 32-bit mode including Average, Box Blur, Gaussian Blur, Motion Blur, Radial Blur, Shape Blur, Surface Blur, Add Noise, Lens Flare, Difference Clouds, Smart Sharpen, Unsharp Mask, Emboss, De-Interlace, NTSC Colors, High Pass, Maximum, Minimum, and Offset.

The **Render > Clouds** filter is now available, but it does not allow you to specify which colors will be used to create the clouds (the version available in 8 and 16-bit images uses foreground/background colors to determine the cloud and background colors.

Edit Menu Commands: The Fill, Stroke, Free Transform, and Transform commands now work with 32-bit images.

File Format Support: You can save 32-bit images into the following file formats: Photoshop, Large Document Format, Radiance, Portable Bit Map, OpenEXR, and TIFF.

Color Modes: You can now convert a 32-bit color image into a 32-bit grayscale image by choosing **Image>Mode>Grayscale**.

Selection Menu Commands: Selections are now better supported with the addition of the following **Select** menu commands: Inverse, Modify Border, Transform Selection, Save Selection and Load Selection.

Many other changes have been made in the new Extended version of Photoshop. Those include 32-bit layers support, more tool support and more. The features available in the extended version of CS3 are beyond the scope of this book.

Misc. Changes

The following changes may not be that noticeable, but they are all welcome improvements:

Brightness/Contrast Improved

In the past, the Brightness/Contrast adjustment was the most crude and destructive adjustment you could find in Photoshop. It was impossible to maintain the full brightness range in an image and was very easy to clip areas to solid black or solid white. That was really unfortunate since it was the easiest adjustment to learn and was the starting point for most beginners when they were learning Photoshop. However, I did find the adjustment to be useful when working on masks, textures and other non-photographic images. The crudeness of the former version of this adjustment caused most Photoshop teachers to insist that beginners never use Brightness/Contrast. That advice is now completely outdated.

The new and improved Brightness/Contrast dialog box doesn't look all that different from the old one, but changes have been made behind the scenes that make all the difference in this feature. The Brightness and Contrast sliders now work using the same ideas that have been used in the Camera Raw dialog box. That means adjusting the Brightness slider on a full-range image will no longer cause clipping in the shadows or highlights because it will concentrate the change on the midtones while leaving black and white areas alone. The Contrast slider is also improved and now applies an S curve to the image, which will also preserve detail and deliver a more pleasing result.

The updated Brightness/Contrast dialog box with Use Legacy checkbox.

In the following examples, the top right image is the original and the others are examples of changes made using the new and legacy settings. The new Brightness/Contrast adjustment will often produce more highlight and shadow detail than the older legacy version.

If you need the Brightness/Contrast dialog box to produce the same type of adjustment as was available in previous versions, turn on the Use Legacy checkbox. This checkbox is sticky, which means that Photoshop will remember the last setting you used the next time you open the dialog box.

A Few Things To Look Out For

Here are a few things you'll need to keep in mind when using the new Brightness/Contrast dialog box:

Adjustment Layers: If you open a file that was created in an earlier version of Photoshop, don't expect any Brightness/Contrast Adjustment Layers to automatically update to use the new features in CS3. Instead, you'll have to double-click on the Adjustment Layer to edit the adjustment and turn off the Use Legacy checkbox if you want the new method to be used.

Backward Compatibility: Saving a file that contains a Brightness/Contrast Adjustment Layer that was created using the new version of the dialog box (with the Use Legacy checkbox turned off), will cause an error message if you attempt to open the image in a previous version of Photoshop. That makes sense because how would the old dialog box be able to interpret a feature that didn't exist when CS2 was released? So, if you plan to open your layered images in older versions of Photoshop, either use the legacy setting, or merge the Adjustment Layer into the image layer before saving the file.

Actions: Existing actions that use the Brightness/Contrast dialog box will be unaffected by this change since they will be applied using legacy settings until you re-record the steps that use the dialog box.

Minor Adjustment Changes

A few of the other adjustment dialog boxes have changed, but the changes are so minute that you might not even notice them:

Levels: The numeric entry fields have been moved so that they are positioned next to the sliders they relate to. This doesn't change the way you use the dialog box at all, so it shouldn't take much to get used to it.

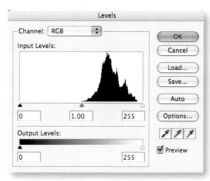

Only cosmetic changes were made to the Levels dialog box.

Channel Mixer: Adjusting the Red, Green and Blue sliders so that the total of the sliders produced a result above 100% would often create an overexposed look. Adobe has simply added a Total readout so you can easily see when the total gets above 100%. This doesn't mean that you should never have it go over 100%; use whatever settings makes your image look its best. It's just nice to use it as a guide to show you when you might want to experiment with lower values. Adobe also changed the default settings used when the Monochrome checkbox is turned on. The new defaults (40% Red, 40% Green and 20% Blue) produce a much better starting point for a grayscale conversion when compared to the old defaults (100% Red, 0% Green, 0% Blue). The Channel Mixer also received the same Presets system that is found in the Black & White and Curves dialog box so you can quickly access frequently used settings.

You can now save presets in the Channel Mixer dialog box. There is also a Total readout and a new default for Monochrome adjustments.

Shadow/Highlight and Variations adjustments (which are not available as Adjustment Layers) can now be applied to a layer non-destructively through a new feature known as Smart Filters.

Smart Filter Adjustments: You can now apply Variations and Shadow/Highlight adjustments to a layer in a non-destructive way (similar to an Adjustment Layer). This new feature is known as Smart Filters and will be discussed in Chapter 6, Layers.

Adobe did themselves proud when they updated Photoshop's adjustments for CS3. They revamped the Brightness/Contrast feature so that beginners wouldn't unsuspectingly ambush their images when using it. We got a wonderful new tool for converting color images to black & white, and Curves junkies got all the bells and whistles they've been writing to Santa about all these years. I'm all smiles here.

Greetings From
he Serengeti

Chapter 5
Tools

ADOBE FOCUSED ON TWO AREAS when revising the tools in CS3: Retouching and Selections. The two shining stars of the show—the Quick Selection tool and Refine Edge palette—introduce an unprecedented level of control and take a lot of the sweat out of tricky selections. Add in the latest retouching features, and you've got some serious fun waiting for you in CS3's Tools palette.

Below is an overview of what we'll be covering in this chapter:

- **Quick Selection Tool:** This slick newcomer has dethroned the Magic Wand in the Tools palette, and was designed for making both basic and complex selections faster and easier than ever before.
- **Refine Edge Palette:** This new secret weapon puts the finishing touches on your selections and masks, allowing you to tweak and polish them with near-surgical precision, regardless of which tool was used to create them.
- **Retouching Tools:** New sampling options have been added to many of the retouching tools making it easier to retouch images made from a complex mix of layers.
- **Clone Source Palette:** This new palette makes the Clone Stamp and Healing Brush tool much more powerful by allowing you to scale and rotate areas of your image to create useful retouching material. It also offers a super helpful little feature that allows you to see a live preview of your clone source.

Where's My Stuff?

Some features you might have used in the last version of Photoshop have changed residence:

- **Magic Wand Tool:** If you're having trouble finding the Magic Wand tool, that's because it's now hiding behind the new Quick Selection tool that appears to the right of (in the double-column toolbar), or below (in the single-column toolbar) the Lasso tool. Just click and hold on that new tool and you'll be able to access the Magic Wand tool.
- **Quick Mask Icon:** The Quick Mask icons near the bottom of the toolbar have been changed into a single icon that now toggles Quick Mask mode on and off. This change was made to accommodate the new single-column toolbar that's available in Photoshop CS3.
- **Feather:** The **Feather** command has been moved from the **Select** menu into a side menu called **Modify**. I'm assuming that's because Adobe is trying to convince you to replace it with the new **Refine Selection** command.

Quick Selection Tool

In previous versions of Photoshop, there were three features that were designed to automate the process of isolating an area from its surroundings—**Magic Wand**, **Color Range**, and **Background Eraser**. The first two choices have always been severely limited in their usefulness, while the third was largely misunderstood and many users didn't even know it existed. All that has changed with the introduction of the new **Quick Selection** tool. By no means is it perfect (the **Extract** command is still much better for hair and other furry subjects), but its approach to making selections is nothing short of revolutionary.

The first stroke was made with a medium-sized brush (stroke shown in red).

Second stroke used to add bottom of log caused reflection to become selected.

A third stroke was used in Subtract mode to remove the reflection from the selection.

When you choose the **Quick Selection** tool, you'll be presented with a standard round brush cursor, but instead of applying color when you paint, it creates a selection that automatically expands to add surrounding areas that are similar in color, contrast and texture to the area over which you are painting. In many situations, the tool will seem to intuitively limit the selection to the boundaries of the object or area you paint within (as long as the edge of the brush never extends beyond the area you want to select). However, there are other situations where complexities in your image can cause this tool to behave less like a clairvoyant and more like a drunken toddler running amok.

The Quick Selection tool's three modes.

Not to worry, once you have a full understanding of how this feature operates, you can easily turn the little monster into a perfectly behaved selection machine. Let's dive in and find out how it works.

Selection Modes: After painting across a portion of your image with the **Quick Selection** tool, you'll notice that once you release the mouse button the tool will automatically switch from creating a selection to adding to the existing selection by changing its mode. The three icons that appear on the left side of the Options bar determine the tool's current mode. The modes available are **New Selection** (left), **Add to Selection** (middle) and **Subtract from Selection** (right). All you have to do to add to an existing selection is release the mouse button and paint over any unselected areas to expand the current selection to include those areas. If no selection is active, then painting in the **Add to Selection** mode will create a new selection.

    Brush:  30 ☐ Sample All Layers ☐ Auto-Enhance Refine Edge...

The Options bar settings available when the Quick Selection tool is active.

Original image before a selection was made.

A few final stokes were made with small brush to touch up edge of the log.

When the tool oversteps the boundaries of the area you are attempting to select, you'll need to click on the **Subtract from Selection** icon in the Options bar and paint over the area you want to remove from the selection.

You'll find that subtracting from a selection in one area will often screw up another area that was otherwise perfectly selected. That's because the Quick Selection tool is only looking at the exact areas over which you've painted and it might decide to change how it handles the surrounding areas based on your latest attempt. When that happens you might need to paint in additional areas using the **Add to Selection** mode in order to produce an acceptable result. You might even have to switch back and forth between the two modes and paint up to a dozen times before you get the selection you need. That might sound complex and time consuming, but

once you get the hang of it, it should only take a few seconds to produce an acceptable selection and the majority of the time the process will be faster than using other selection methods.

Brush Sizes: You can use a different sized brush for each stroke you apply with this tool (press] or [to change your brush size using the keyboard). Use small brushes in very constricted areas and a large brush when painting over broad areas. I find that hard-edged brushes usually produce the best results (you can change the Hardness setting of your brush by holding **Shift** and pressing] and [on your keyboard).

Sample All Layers: With default settings, the **Quick Selection** tool will only look at the active layer when determining what should be selected (as if the other layers don't exist). If the area you are attempting to select is made out of more than one layer, be sure to turn on the **Sample All Layers** checkbox in the Options bar so that the tool can look at all the layers when determining which areas should be selected.

Auto-Enhance: Turning on the **Auto-Enhance** checkbox in the Options bar will cause the Quick Selection tool to spend more time calculating the edge of a selection in an effort to improve its quality and create a truer, more precise selection. It won't look any different while you are painting, but you'll encounter a slight pause when you release the mouse button before you see the refined results. Working with that option turned off can produce the opposite of what you are trying to accomplish: jaggy edges in places that should be smooth; soft edges that should be crisp; or crisp edges at the edge of an object that is out of focus or in motion and would be better with a soft-edged selection. Turning the checkbox off will produce what you might call a "quick and dirty selection" whereas turning it on will produce a more refined edge.

When working on small images, the performance penalty of using the **Auto-Enhance** feature is small enough that it makes sense to leave it on all the time. With larger, higher resolution images, the performance penalty might be too frustrating to deal with. In that case, turn off the **Auto-Enhance** option when creating a selection and then turn it on and paint across what is already selected (while using the **Add to Selection** mode) to enhance the entire selection. That will not produce as refined of a result as leaving the checkbox turned on the entire time, but it can give you a good compromise between speed and quality.

The Refine Edge dialog box can be accessed from the Select menu. Mousing over each slider (without clicking) will cause a description of the slider to appear at the bottom of the dialog box.

Refine Edge's default settings did not produce an acceptable result.

Result of zeroing out the Refine Edge settings.

The Auto-Enhance feature uses the technology that's available in the new **Select>Refine Edge** command (along with other wizardry), so let's see how that command can be used to further improve an existing selection.

Refine Edge

The **Refine Edge** command (accessed via the **Edit** menu, or the **Refine Edge** button in the Options bar of all selection tools) is designed to improve the edge quality of any selection or mask. Let's look at the features available one at a time:

Radius: Determines the complexity of the edge of the selection. Higher settings are necessary on complex or soft-edged objects, while lower settings are appropriate for simple, crisp-edged objects.

Contrast: Determines how abrupt the selection edge will be. When a high Radius setting is needed for a complex edge, you might need to increase the **Contrast** setting to prevent the edge from become too soft. On an out of focus or in motion object, you might need to lower the **Contrast** setting to maintain a soft edged selection.

Smooth: This setting will cause any sharp corners to become rounded, which can simplify an edge that is more complex than what you want.

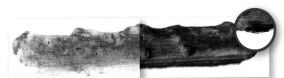

Left: Radius too high. Right: Radius just right.

Result of changing Contrast setting to 50%.

Result of changing Smooth setting to 2.

Result of changing Feather setting to 1.0.

Feather: This setting will generically soften the edge of a selection (without taking into consideration the edge quality of the image itself) in the same way as applying the **Feather** command that is found under the **Select>Modify** menu. I find that using very low numbers (like .2) can often help when making selections on very low resolution images.

Contract/Expand: Moving this slider toward the left will make a selection smaller, while moving it to the right will make it larger (similar to increasing or decreasing the amount of air in a balloon). It's like applying the **Contract** and **Expand** commands that are found under the **Select>Modify** menu, but the adjustment is measured as a percentage instead of in pixels, which allows for finer control over the selection edge.

Preview Mode: The five icons found near the bottom of the Refine Edge dialog box determine which type of preview will be used. From left to right, the choices available include: **Standard**, **Quick Mask**, **On Black**, **On White**, **Mask**. Let's take a look at how each one functions.

Standard Mode will display the changes as a normal selection edge (often referred to as "marching ants"). This is useful when you want to see the entire image without any color overlays and are not concerned with how hard or soft the selection edge is.

Quick Mask Mode will display the selection using the same settings as the **Quick Mask Mode** that is available near the bottom of Photoshop's toolbar. Default settings make it so that non-selected areas of the image are covered with a red overlay, while selected areas remain unchanged.

Standard mode shows a "marching ants" selection.

Quick Mask mode displays non-selected areas as a red overlay.

On Black mode displays non-selected areas as solid black.

On White mode displays non-selected areas as solid white.

Mask mode displays the selection as it would appear in a mask.

Double-clicking the Quick Mask Mode icon will display this dialog box.

You can change the color and opacity of the overlay by double-clicking on the **Quick Mask Mode** icon to access its options dialog box. The **Color Indicates** setting will determine where the color is overlaid on the image. The **Masked Areas** setting will cause the non-selected areas to be overlaid with color, while the **Selected Areas** setting will place the color over areas that are selected. You can also change the color of the overlay and how much you can see through it by clicking on the color swatch (which will produce a color picker) and adjusting the **Opacity** setting.

NOTE

On Any Color
If you find the On White and On Black options to be too limiting (because you want to see what an object would look like when pasted onto a specific color), consider using Quick Mask Mode while setting the Opacity to 100% and using a custom color. That way you can see what an object would look like on any colored background.

That's useful when the image you're working with contains a lot of red, orange, or yellow areas, which makes a red overlay difficult to see.

This mode (along with all the modes that follow) has a huge advantage over **Standard Mode** because it gives you the truest representation of your selection edge.

On Black Mode will fill non-selected areas with solid black. Adjusting the sliders until the edge smoothly blends into the black background should give you a pretty good idea of what the image would look like if you pasted it onto a dark background.

On White Mode will fill non-selected areas with solid white. Adjusting the sliders until the edge smoothly blends into the white background should give you a good indication of what the image would look like if you pasted it onto a bright background.

Mask Mode will display selected areas as white and non-selected areas as black, while shades of gray represent transition areas. This is useful when you want to determine if an area is fully selected. If you see single-pixel specks in this mode (often referred to as twinklers since they flash when viewed as a normal selection), increase the **Smooth** setting to get rid of them.

The **Refine Edge** command is not limited to modifying a selection. It can also be used on any Layer Mask. Just choose **Select>Refine Edge** when the Layer Mask is active.

Retouching Tools

There are no new retouching tools in Photoshop CS3, but there are some new options that make the existing tools much more useful.

Sample Mode

In previous versions of Photoshop, most of the retouching tools were limited to sampling from either the active layer, or all layers. It's a common practice to create a new, empty layer before retouching an image in order to preserve the contents of the original image so you could always get back to the original at a later time. In order to perform retouching on an empty layer, you had to turn on the **Sample All Layers** checkbox in the Options bar to allow the retouching tools to see (or sample) the contents of the underlying layer, which contained the original image.

A common problem with the old method was encountered when performing retouching on a layer that was placed in a document that contained Adjustment Layers. If the layer that contained the retouching was located below an Adjustment Layer, sampling from all the layers caused the retouching tools to sample from a version of the image that already had the adjustment applied, but the result was placed on a layer below the Adjustment Layer, which caused it to be applied twice. To avoid this problem, it was necessary to hide all the Adjustment Layers that appeared above the layer on which the retouching was applied. That often had the consequence of making it more difficult to retouch the image because the original image might have been overly light or dark before the adjustments were applied. It was also difficult to judge how the resulting retouching would affect the final image, because turning the adjustments back on would often expose problems that were caused by the retouching. Sound messy? It was, but thankfully Adobe has deep-sixed that particular can of worms by giving us a much better, and safer, method for sampling.

The Options bar settings for the Clone Stamp tool (the Ignore Adjustment Layers icon is found on the far right).

In Photoshop CS3, Adobe replaced the **Sample All Layers** checkbox with the new **Ignore Adjustment Layers** icon and **Sample** pop-up menu, which offers the choices of **Current Layer**, **Current and Below**, and **All Layers**. Let's take a look at each option that's available and when it is useful.

Current Layer: This setting is useful when the layer you need to retouch interacts with other layers using blending modes or the blending sliders and you want to limit the retouching so that it only applies to the information in the active layer.

The Sample menu from the Options bar.

Original image before Adjustment Layers were added.

Result of applying three Adjustment layers and a layer that uses a blending mode to interact with the underlying image.

Current & Below: This setting is useful when applying retouching on layers that are positioned below an Adjustment Layer, or layers that have blending modes applied. This is the setting I use in most situations. I will usually create an empty layer directly above the layer I'd like to retouch and then use this setting to apply the retouching. I'll also link the two layers together so they will move together. I'm really disappointed that this choice is not available when using the Spot Healing Brush and Patch tool since it would make them much more useful.

Retouching applied using the Current & Below setting allows you to place the retouching on a separate layer below any Adjustment Layers.

All Layers: Use this setting when the image is too complex to work in a flexible manner (possibly you can't figure out which is the right layer to retouch) and you're pretty sure you won't be making future changes to the underlying layers.

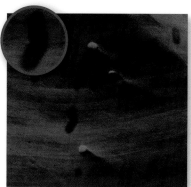

Retouching applied using the All Layers setting causes the adjustments to be applied twice.

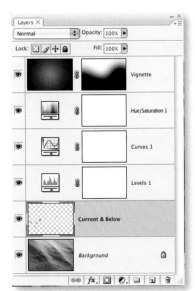

Clone Source Palette

The new Clone Source palette (which can be accessed from the **Window** menu) is home to a multitude of new features that make the Healing brush and Clone Stamp tools much more versatile. And, for the first time, a nifty overlay feature allows us to effectively preview the clone source before committing to cloning, so the days of "eyeballing" it when trying to align content are over.

Clone Source Icons

At the top of the palette you'll find five icons that are used to store different clone sources. If you change which icon is active—before **Option-clicking** (Mac), or **Alt-clicking** (Win) within an image to define a source—you can easily switch back to a previously used clone source in the future by clicking on the respective icon.

Ignore Adjustment Layers: I have no idea when you'd want to use this setting (it's activated by clicking on the icon that appears to the right of the **Sample** pop-up menu). It was added early in the development of CS3 and at that time it sounded like a good idea since many users were complaining that Adjustment Layers were applied twice when using the old **Sample All Layers** checkbox (which was my main complaint about previous versions). I don't find it to be useful because it doesn't make sense to ignore layers of any kind that appear below the layer on which the retouching is being performed as using that setting has the potential to change the image in unexpected ways. I find that the new **Current and Below** sampling option solves the problem that the **Ignore Adjustment Layers** icon was originally designed to address and does it in a much more versatile fashion.

The **Sample** pop-up menu is a nice addition in CS3, but it's not the star of the retouching show. That is reserved for the new **Clone Source** palette, which gives us a treasure trove of little gems to add to our arsenal of retouching tools.

I find the Clone Source icons to be very useful when I'm using multiple clone sources to reconstruct a complex area (like the area behind the palm tree shown in this chapter). It allows me to quickly switch back and forth between clone sources which makes it easier to produce a complex result that is created from multiple sources.

The Clone Source palette.

The clone source icons are essential when performing retouching on a video source because they allow you to retouch using data from different frames of the video source. Editing video is only possible in the Extended version of Photoshop CS3, so it is beyond the scope of this book.

Let's skip over the **Offset**, **Scale** and **Rotation** settings for now and talk about the **Show Overlay** settings that are found at the bottom of the palette. We'll look at things in a bottom-to-top order since the overlay is essential when attempting to adjust the **Offset**, **Scale** and **Rotation** settings.

Show Overlay

Turning on the **Show Overlay** checkbox will cause Photoshop to place a ghosted version of the clone source over your image so you can see how it aligns with the underlying image. This is mainly useful when you need to align content in the source and destination areas.

Turning on the **Auto Hide** checkbox will hide the overlay the moment you click the mouse button and start to apply the retouching.

You can also hold **Shift** and **Option** (Mac), or **Shift** and **Alt** (Win) to temporarily display the overlay. I find that I use the temporary overlay for most of my retouching jobs and only manually turn on the overlay when I have a limited amount of source material from which to clone (the overlay helps prevent you from reaching past the edge of good source material because it allows you to see exactly where it ends).

The **Opacity** setting determines how strong the overlay will be compared to the underlying image. If you find the overlay to be difficult to see, increase the **Opacity** setting. If you find it difficult to make out the underlying image, then lower the **Opacity** setting.

The **Mode** pop-up menu is found directly below the **Opacity** setting. It allows you to determine how the overlay should interact with the underlying image. This can be useful in the following situations:

The Overlay Mode menu in the Clone Source palette.

Original image showing clone source location at left.

Normal @ 50%

Normal @ 50%, invert

Difference @ 100%

Difference @ 100%, invert

Lighten @ 100%

Darken @ 100%

Precise Alignment: When you need to precisely align a clone source with the underlying image, you'll most likely want to turn off the **Invert** checkbox, set the **Opacity** to 100% and experiment with the **Mode** pop-up menu to find the setting that produces the most useful overlay. Lighten mode is useful when the object you are trying to retouch out of an image is darker than the clone source that's being used to retouch the area (just as Darken mode is useful when the object is lighter than the clone source). Difference mode will cause areas that align perfectly to appear as black while misaligned areas appear as different colors.

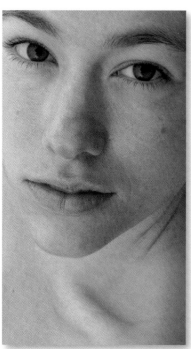

Original image before adjustments or retouching has been performed.

Three separate layers were used to apply retouching: 1) Moles removed with Healing Brush, 2) Neck Wrinkles removed with Healing Brush using a layer set to Lighten mode, 3) Face retouched using Healing Brush on a layer with opacity set to 75%.

Six adjustment layers were used to enhance the image. The following areas were changed:
1) Contrast added to eyes,
2) Saturation increased in eyes,
3) Blue lessened on edge of eye,
4) Saturation lowered in neck to help face separate from neck,
5) Lips made darker,
6) Overall contrast boosted.

Retouching with Blending Modes: It's not uncommon to apply facial retouching using the Lighten or Darken blending modes. The respective preview modes are useful in this situation because they provide an exact preview of what you'd achieve if you were to apply the retouching using those modes.

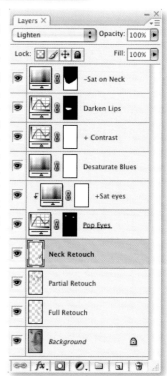

Layers palette view of image shown above.

Offset

The **Offset** setting will reflect how far you've moved horizontally (the X value) and vertically (the Y value) between where you **Option-clicked** (Mac), or **Alt-clicked** (Win) to define the clone source and where you applied the retouching. This is nice because you can make fine adjustments to the positioning if you notice that the source does not perfectly align with the area you are attempting to retouch. When this happens I usually type **Command-Z** (Mac), or **Ctrl-Z** (Win) to undo the retouching and without moving my mouse, hold **Shift-Option** (Mac), or **Shift-Alt** (Win) and use the **Arrow Keys** to adjust the Offset value while watching the overlay (which appears when holding the two keys mentioned above) to see when the clone source aligns with the underlying image before clicking again to retouch the area.

Scale

The **Scale** setting is useful when the area you are cloning from is of a different size than the area you plan to retouch (possibly because it's at a different distance from the camera). When that's the case, **Option-click** (Mac), or **Alt-click** (Win) on the area you want to clone from, and hold **Shift** and **Option** (Mac), or **Shift** and **Alt** (Win) which will cause the overlay to be visible, and then use the bracket keys (] and [) to change the Scale setting until the clone source matches the size of the area you plan to retouch. Once the overlay image matches the underlying image, release the keys you were holding and click to start retouching the image.

> **NOTE**
>
> **Keyboard Commands**
> The keyboard shortcuts used for changing the **Offset**, **Scale** and **Rotate** settings will not work if one of the text fields in the **Clone Source** palette is active (you'll be typing text in the active field instead). When a text field is active, press **Return** or **Enter** to have Photoshop accept the entry (you'll have to dismiss an error message if you entered unacceptable characters) which will allow the keyboard shortcuts to control the settings in the **Clone Source** palette.

To flip the image horizontally or vertically, enter a negative number into the **Scale** setting. This is useful when working on a portrait of someone who wears glasses where one side of the glasses has glare while the other is clear. By setting the Width to -100% you will apply a horizontally flipped version of the clone source, which will allow you to clone from the clear eye to replace the glare in the other eye.

Rotate

The **Rotate** feature has a multitude of uses including straightening heads and body parts in group shots and cloning from vertical edges to repair horizontal ones. You can hold **Shift** and **Option** (Mac), or **Shift** and **Alt** (Win) and use the greater than and less than keys (**>** and **<**) to adjust the **Rotate** setting.

The **Offset**, **Scale** and **Rotate** settings are a powerful combination when you need to retouch using a source from a second photograph that might have been taken from a different vantage point than the image that is being retouched. It's also essential when cloning from an area that is very close to the area that will be retouched. By flipping the source material horizontally, vertically and rotating the source, it will be more difficult to recognize a repeated pattern of similar detail, which has always been a challenge with cloning.

Original image before retouching has been performed.

Palm tree, parking meter and small sign removed.

In the example above, the palm tree was removed from the right side of the photograph using a variety of settings in the **Clone Source** palette. To start, the **Width** setting was set to -100 to flip the photograph horizontally. The **Width** and **Height** settings were then fine-tuned until two areas near the palm tree turned solid black to indicate they were perfectly aligned. The **Angle** setting was also changed to create a more precise fit. This source was used to retouch the top portion of the palm tree.

Difference mode overlay used to retouch the top portion of the palm tree. Areas on the right side of the image align as indicated by solid black (see red arrows).

Clone Source setting used to retouch the top portion of the palm tree.

The middle portion of the tree trunk was retouched using a non-distorted source from the area to the left of the tree.

The base of the tree was retouched using part of the railing that is found to the left of the tree (its sample point was used as an example in the overlay section earlier in this chapter).

Misc. Changes?

There really is only one other change in the Tools palette that we haven't covered so far:

Expanded Sample Size: The following features use the **Sample Size** setting that is found in the Options bar when the **Eyedropper** tool is active: **Eyedropper** tool (both in the toolbar and the ones found in Levels and Curves), **Magic Wand** tool, **Magic Eraser** tool, **Paintbucket** tool. With the ever-increasing resolution of digital cameras, the former choices of Point Sample (meaning a single pixel), 3x3 Average and 5x5 Average, were simply not enough to accurately sample a general area while averaging in the effect of noise and other artifacts in the image.

To accommodate our evolving digital images, Adobe has expanded the range of **Sample Sizes** available to include **11 by 11 Average**, **31 by 31 Average**, **51 by 51 Average**, and **101 by 101 Average**. That should satisfy people who work with especially high resolution images. Just be careful because using a high setting can radically change how the **Magic Wand** tool works (since it's averaging such a large area instead of only sampling from a single pixel). I really wish Adobe would allow for different **Sample Size** settings for all of the tools that use the setting so I could have a very sensitive **Magic Wand** (with a **Sample Size** of **3 by 3 Average**), while using a much higher **Sample Size** setting for the **Eyedropper** tools found in the **Curves** dialog box.

Most of the new features we covered here come with a relatively small learning curve, and the time you invest in getting to know them will quickly result in big dividends. Remember, even when you think a new option or feature might be small and insignificant, you will often find its true power when you use it in combination with another tool. This is especially true of the tools described in this chapter. Overall, I've found that making selections and performing retouching to be a much more enjoyable process in Photoshop CS3 and I hope you have an equally satisfying experience as you play with the new toys.

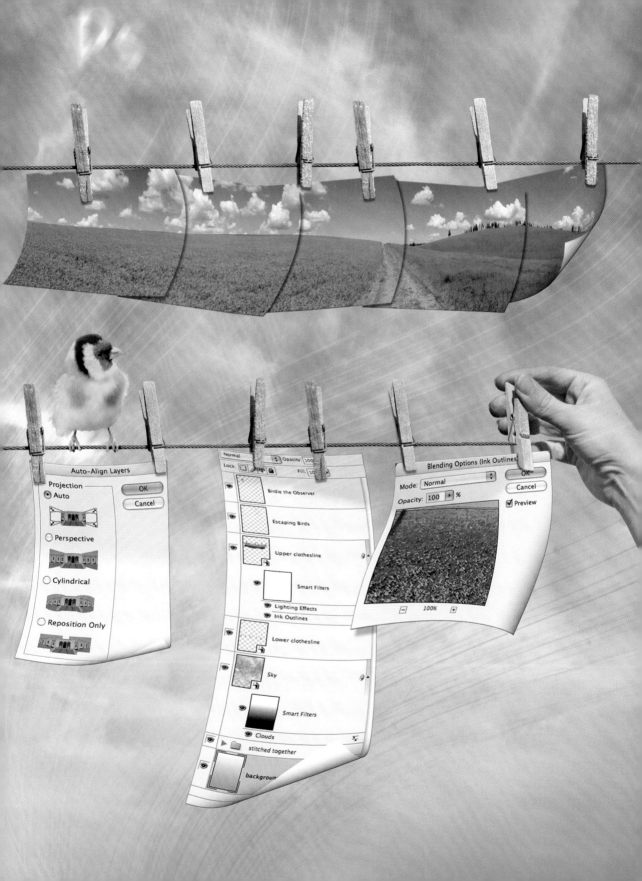

Chapter 6
Layers

I F THERE'S ONE STAND OUT, blow-your-mind feature in Photoshop CS3, it's got to be the new Auto-Align and Auto-Blend Layers commands. It's as if they've imported something from 2017 to make it work. But that's not all there is to get excited about when it comes to layers in CS3: we now have non-destructive filters and some new blending modes to play with.

Below is an overview of what we'll be covering in this chapter:

- **Smart Filters:** For the first time in Photoshop you can non-destructively apply filters to a layer. Once Smart Filters have been applied you can quickly copy them between layers and edit the settings as many times as you want to without hurting even one innocent little pixel.
- **New Blending Modes:** The new Lighter Color and Darker Color blending modes are welcome additions, but not a radical departure from the existing modes.
- **Auto-Align Layers:** A dazzling new feature (especially when combined with the new Auto-Blend Layers command) that allows anyone to create near-perfect panoramas. Even shots taken handheld and in automatic mode will often produce stunning results.
- **Auto-Blend Layers:** Another "wow" feature that seamlessly blends multiple images and aligns their edges with amazing precision.

Where's My Stuff?

When it comes to the Layers palette, Adobe pretty much left well enough alone, so if you're still recovering from the CS2 makeover, you can breathe a sigh of relief. The only thing that might make you think twice is that the Layer Effects icon is no longer a black circle; it's now the letters "fx." If you can handle that, there's nothing else standing between you and a brilliant future with CS3 Layers, so let's jump right into the new stuff and get started.

Smart Filters

In previous versions of Photoshop, filters were limited to affecting a single layer. Applying them was thought of as a destructive process because saving and closing the document afterward would permanently change the layer to which the filter was applied. Because of this, many people got in the habit of first duplicating the layer (to which they wanted to apply a filter) so they would always have a copy of the original to fall back on. In complex, multi-layered documents, this meant creating a "merged-duplicate" by typing **Shift-Op-**

tion-**Command-E** (Mac), or **Shift-Alt-Ctrl-E** (Win). This cumbersome process severely limited the ability to make future edits to the underlying layers (you'd have to trash the merged layer, make changes to the underlying layers, then create a new "merged-duplicate," apply the filters again and then try to remember the filter settings that were previously applied). Well, we can kiss the old way goodbye, because the oh-so-wonderful CS3 Smart Filters have come to save our bacon.

Smart Filters allow you to non-destructively apply one or more filters to one or more layers while maintaining the ability to make changes to the individual layers, edit the filter settings at any time, and specify a blending mode for each filter (just like using the **Edit>Fade** command in CS2). And if that doesn't twirl your propeller, you can also apply a mask to a Smart Filter.

Applying Smart Filters

Before applying a Smart Filter, you must first select one or more layers and choose **Filter>Convert for Smart Filters**, or **Layer>Smart Objects>Convert to Smart Object**. That will effectively move the layers into a special file that is represented by the resulting Smart Object layer (which looks as if the selected layers were merged together). This special file is embedded into the document that contains the Smart Object layer (as indicated by the document icon on the layer thumbnail) and can be accessed by double-clicking on the thumbnail image for the layer in the Layers palette.

NOTE

Smart Objects
The concept of Smart Objects was introduced in Photoshop CS2. For more in-depth coverage of this feature, check out the Smart Objects chapter in my book *Photoshop CS2: Up to Speed*.

Left: Normal layer thumbnail, Right: Smart Object thumbnail.

When a Smart Object layer is active, any filters applied will be considered Smart Filters and will appear in the Layers palette in a list below the Smart Object layer.

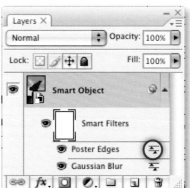

Smart Filters appear in a list below the Smart Object layer to which they are attached. Double-click the circled area to access the filter's Blending Options.

Here are some of the things you can do with a Smart Filter:

Edit Filter Settings: Double-click on the name of any filter listed below a Smart Object to change the filter settings. When the filter dialog box is open, you will only see the result of filters that appear below the one you are editing. Any filters above it in the stack will show up after you click OK in the filter dialog box. Double-clicking filters that do not offer settings but produce different results each time they are applied (like the Clouds filter) will cause the filter to be recalculated.

NOTE

Collapsed Filter List
The list of Smart Filters applied to a layer can be collapsed and expanded by clicking the small arrow that appears on the right edge of a layer that has Smart Filters applied. Choose Palette Options from the Side menu of the Layers palette and turn off the Expand New Effects checkbox if you'd prefer the Smart Filters list to be collapsed by default.

Set Blending Options: If you double-click the small icon that appears to the right of any Smart Filter, you will be presented with Blending Mode choices (like Multiply and Screen) and Opacity that can be used to change the way the filter interacts with the image.

Double-click the icon to the right of a Smart Filter to specify blending options.

Filter progression divided into quarters, clockwise from upper left: Original, Median filter in Normal mode, Find Edges in Normal mode, Find Edges changed to Multiply mode.

Change Order: You can drag the name of a Smart Filter up or down in the list of filters to change the order in which they are applied. The filters will be applied from bottom to top. Be forewarned: Photoshop can take awhile to update the screen when you re-order the filters because it has to re-calculate the results of all the filters in order to display the results.

The left half of this image shows the Median filter applied first and then the Find Edges filter applied in Multiply mode. The right half shows the result of reversing the order of the filters.

Hide/Show Filter: You can click on the eyeball icon that appears to the left of a Smart Filter to disable and re-enable a Smart Filter (drag down the eyeball column to turn off multiple eyeballs). You can also drag the name of a Smart Filter to the mini trash can that appears at the bottom of the Layers palette to permanently delete a Smart Filter, or drag the words "Smart Filters" to the trash to delete all the Smart Filters applied to the layer.

Move/Copy Between Layers: To move a Smart Filter, you can click on its name and drag it to another Smart Object layer. To copy it, just hold **Option** (Mac), or **Alt** (Win) while you're dragging. You can also drag a Smart Filter to another document as long as the active layer in the destination document has been converted into a Smart Object ahead of time.

Mask Filters: You can click on the mask that appears to the left of the words "Smart Filters" to make it active (as indicated by corner markings) and then paint with black to reveal the unfiltered version of the layer. The mask will affect all of the Smart Filters attached to the active layer.

Left: Mask active. Right: Mask not active.

The Radial Blur filter was applied to this image as a Smart Filter and then black was added to the mask to prevent the filter from affecting the center portion of the image.

If you'd like to apply a separate mask to each filter, you'll have to use nested Smart Objects. Start by applying one filter and painting on the associated mask. Next, choose **Layer>Smart Objects>Convert to Smart Object** to embed the first Smart Object into a fresh one. Finally, apply a filter to the newly created Smart Object and paint on its mask. You can repeat this process for as many filters as you need to apply. To edit the original content, you'll have to double-click on each progressive Smart Object until you've gone deep enough to locate the original layer. It's not the most elegant solution, but it's nice to have as an option.

The filter mask works just like any other layer mask in that you can **Shift-click** on the mask to temporarily disable it or **Option-click** (Mac), or **Alt-click** the mask to view its contents. One thing to keep in mind when using the Move tool to move masks on Smart Filters and/or Smart Objects: when a Smart Filter is active (as indicated by corner marks on the filter mask thumbnail), you can move just the filter mask. When the Smart Object layer is active (as indicated by corner marks on the image thumbnail) both the image and the filter mask will move together. However, if you have a mask on the Smart Object layer itself, and move that, you will find that only the mask will move, leaving the image where it was.

NOTE

Mask Overlay?

Pressing \ (which usually displays a mask as a colored overlay) does not work on Smart Filter masks. You can achieve a similar result by toggling the mask's visibility manually in the Channels palette.

Edit Smart Object Contents: If you'd like to edit the layers that make up the Smart Object, double-click on the thumbnail image for the layer in the Layers palette. That will cause the layers contained within the Smart Object to appear as a separate document. When you are done modifying the layers, choose **File>Save** and close the window that contains the layers to save them back into the document they are contained within. This means that you can do things like apply a filter to text and still be able to edit the text.

Rasterize Layer: Choosing **Layer>Rasterize>Smart Object** will merge the layers contained within the Smart Object and permanently apply any Smart Filters attached to the layer. This command is necessary for those times when you need to send a layered file to someone who owns an older version of Photoshop that doesn't support Smart Filters, or when you need to apply a filter that is not available as a Smart Filter, or you're just trying to reduce your file size. The following filters cannot be applied as Smart Filters: Extract, Liquify, Pattern Maker, Vanishing Point, and Digimarc.

Applying Adjustments Via Smart Filters

Filters aren't the only thing you can apply using the Smart Filters feature. You can also apply **Shadow/Highlight** and **Variations** via the **Image>Adjustments** menu. This might seem odd since Adjustment Layers are designed for applying adjustments. The reason you have to apply those two adjustments through Smart Filters is due to a limitation in how Adjustment Layers work–they must be able to calculate an adjustment without having to compare one area of an image to another. The Shadow/Highlight and Variations adjustments rely on comparing one area to another to calculate their results and therefore can't be used as Adjustment Layers.

NOTE

Bit Depth & Filters

Many of Photoshop's filters (as well as some adjustments that can be applied via Smart Filters) are not available when working with 16 or 32-bit images.

Converting a layer into a Smart Object while in 16-bit mode and then converting the parent document to 8-bit mode will not convert the contents of the Smart Object into the lower bit depth.

Smart Filter Tips & Tricks

Now that you've been introduced to Smart Filters, let's explore some unique ways in which they can be used.

Adjust Layer: Adjustments cannot be applied directly to a Smart Object (with two exceptions that I'll mention later in this chapter). To adjust a Smart Object, choose the adjustment you desire from the **Layer>New Adjustment Layer** menu and turn on the **Use Previous Layer for Clipping Mask** checkbox, which will cause the Adjustment Layer to only affect the layer that was active at the time the adjustment was applied.

The down-pointing arrow next to this Adjustment Layer indicates that it will only affect the underlying layer.

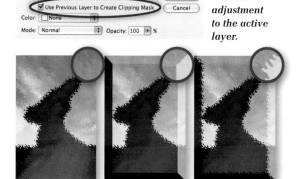

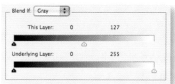

The checkbox limits an adjustment to the active layer.

Blending Slider settings used to remove background on image shown above.

Left: Original image with Ripple Smart Filter applied. Middle: Bevel & Emboss Layer Effect applied to Smart Object layer. Right: Layer Effect applied to Smart Object contents.

Left: Warped Smart Object. Middle: Radial Blur (spin setting) Filter applied to the warped layer. Right: Filter applied to layer contained within the Smart Object.

Add Layer Effects: Any normal Layer Effects (like Bevel & Emboss, or Drop Shadow) added to a Smart Object layer will apply to the layer after any Smart Filters. If you'd rather have them apply before the filters, be sure to add the Layer Effects before converting the layer into a Smart Object.

Apply Blending Sliders: Blending Sliders (accessed by choosing **Layer> Layer Style> Blending Options**) will apply to the after-filter result (you can edit the filter setting and see a live filter/sliders preview). Take note: Layer Effects will be applied *after* the filter and will ignore how the blending sliders are shaping the layer.

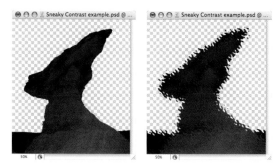

Left: Background removed using Blending sliders. Right: Result of applying Smart Filter to layer.

Apply Transformations: You can apply the choices found under the **Edit>Transform** menu to layers that have Smart Filters applied and still edit the filter settings later. The filter's effects will be hidden while transforming to make the screen update faster. The transformation will apply after the filter's effect has been applied. If you want the filter to apply before the transformation, double-click on the Smart Object and apply the filter to the layer that is contained within the Smart Object.

Pre-Filter Masks: Adding a Layer Mask to a layer that has Smart Filters will apply *after* the filters have been applied. If you need to mask the image before the filters are applied, edit the contents of the Smart Object and add the mask within the Smart Object.

Layer Retrieval: Once you've converted multiple layers into a Smart Object, there is no command that will pull those layers back out of the Smart Object. To extract layers from a Smart Object, double-click the Smart Object so you can see the layers contained within it and use the Move tool to drag the layers back to the original file.

Mix Filters & Adjustments: You can intermix Smart Filters with Shadow/Highlight and Variations adjustments (which are applied to a Smart Object via the **Image>Adjustments** menu). This can be useful when you want to remove the color cast created by the Emboss filter (apply Variations to lower the saturation until no color is left).

Forced Update: If you're used to applying the Displace filter (which requires an external file) or the Lens Blur or Lighting Effects filters (which can use the content of a channel to change the way the filter is applied), you'll be glad to know that you can force an update of the Smart Filter results after modifying the file or channel the filter is referencing. Hold **Shift** and **Option** (Mac), or **Alt** (Win) and click on the **Smart Filters** title that appears just below the layer's name in the Layers palette.

Enabling 3rd Party Filters: The Smart Filters feature does not support 3rd party filters you may have purchased, but don't despair. If you're dying to use a filter that is not supported by Smart Filters, you can use the script that is found on the CD that ships with Photoshop CS3. It's located in the **Scripts/JavaScript** folder and is called **EnableAllPluginsForSmartFilters.jsx**. Running the script will allow you to enable any 3rd party filter to work with Smart Objects. You'll have to be cautious though because there is the potential for problems with filters that were not designed to be used with this feature. Examples include:

Creating Duplicate Layers: Some 3rd party filters create a duplicate layer, which will not work when using Smart Filters.

Filters That Rely on Layer Shape: Many filters that distort the contents of a layer can be thrown off when a layer that contains a Smart Filter is rotated or transformed.

Smart Filters are an awesome addition to Photoshop, and when it comes to what you can do in the Layers palette in CS3, it just keeps on getting better. Lick your chops and we'll move on to the next batch of goodies.

New Blending Modes

Photoshop CS3 sports two new blending modes– Lighter Color and Darker Color. They are very similar to the Lighten and Darken modes with one important difference that can only be explained by describing both the older and newer modes in detail:

Lighten & Darken Modes: Behind the scenes, your image is made out of a mix of red, green and blue light. The Darken and Lighten modes look at those colors individually, picking the lighter or darker version of each color when calculating the end result. That means that combining a brown color that contains 70% Red, 50% Green and 10% Blue with a blue color that contains 10% Red, 60% Green and 70% Blue in Lighten mode will choose the individual Red, Green and Blue numbers that are highest to produce the result (since higher numbers mean more light and therefore the lighter version of each color). The end result would be a dull purple color containing 70% Red, 60% Green and 70% Blue. Combining the two colors using Darken mode would produce a green color containing 10% Red, 50% Green and 10% Blue.

Photoshop CS3 offers two new blending modes: Lighter Color and Darker Color.

Colors mentioned in the text combined using Darken (left) and Lighten modes (right).
Note: The backgrounds had to be changed to make sure the colors being compared were lighter or darker than their respective backgrounds.

Colors mentioned in the text combined using Darker Color (left) and Lighter Color modes (right).

Lighter Color & Darker Color Modes: These modes compare the total amount of light in each color to determine which color is lighter or darker and then use the full Red, Green and Blue values for whichever color was lightest or darkest, depending on the mode you've chosen. In the example used above, adding up the percentages for Red, Green and Blue would give you 130% for the brown color and 140% for the blue color. If the two colors were combined using Lighter Color mode, the result would be exactly the same as the blue color that you started with. That's because the total amount of light in that color is higher than the brown color it was being compared to. Using the same line of reasoning, combining the colors using Darker Color mode would produce the brown color you started with since it contains less light than the blue color.

The main difference between these two sets of modes is that the Lighter Color/Darker Color set will produce an end result that looks exactly like the color found in one of the two layers that are being blended, while the Lighten/Darken group will always produce a third color that is created from combining highest or lowest values of the red, green and blue light from which the layers are made.

Now that you know the technical difference between the two sets of modes, let's take a look at the real-world differences and figure out when they should be used.

Replacing Areas with A Single Color

In the example below, I wanted to replace all the dark areas of the image with a solid dark blue color. I knew that using Lighten or Lighter Color mode would do that as long as the color I chose to use was lighter than the areas I wanted to replace and darker than the areas I didn't want to replace. In this case, I ended up using Lighter Color mode since I did not want any intermediate colors to appear in the image. Lighten mode always produces a mix of the two colors being compared, whereas Lighter Color mode gives you one color or the other, but never a mix of the two.

Top left: Original.
Top right: Color applied in Lighten mode.
Lower left: Color applied in Lighter Color mode.
Above: Split image, top=Lighten, bottom=Lighter Color. Notice the slight color difference in the darkest portion of the images.

Partial Black & White Conversions

The new Black & White adjustment removes all the color from an image. We can change that by using the Lighten Color or Darken Color Blending mode.

In the example below, I chose **Layer>Adjustment Layers>Black & White** and specified the Darker Color blending mode so that any areas of the Black & White conversion that produced a lighter result than the original image would not affect the image. I adjusted the sliders in the Black & White dialog box until the entire image had no color (by darkening each color a little) and then for the area in which I wanted to retain color I just moved the appropriate slider toward the right to brighten it until that color appeared.

Inverting Bright Areas

In the example below, I wanted to create an unusual image by inverting only the bright areas of the image. I accomplished that by choosing **Layer>Adjustment Layers>Invert** and setting the **Blending Mode** pop-up menu to **Lighter Color**, which prevented any areas from becoming darker. Since inverting usually makes dark areas bright and bright areas dark, this limited the change to the bright areas of the image.

If I had used the Darken blending mode, the colors in the transition area would have produced a color shift as can be seen in the door and roof line of the example below. In general, I use Lighten Color and Darken Color modes when I want to prevent these color shifts.

Creating an Adjustment Layer in Darker Color mode.

Top left:
Original image.
Top right:
Black & White adjustment applied using Normal mode.
Bottom right:
Black & White adjustment applied using the Darker Color mode caused colors that were lightened in the black and white conversion to not affect the image.

Top left: Original. Top right: Inverted version.
Lower left: Invert layer set to Darken mode.
Lower right: Invert layer set to Darker Color mode.

Remapping Colors in Bright Areas

In the photo below, I noticed that the church was quite a bit darker than the sky. It gave me an opportunity to test out the Brighter Color blending mode to limit a Gradient Map adjustment to see if I could get it to only affect the church.

I started by choosing **Layer>Adjustment Layers> Gradient Map** and setting the **Blending Mode** pop-up menu to **Lighter Color**. That prevented the adjustment from darkening the image. I then chose one of the default gradients and clicked in the middle of the gradient preview to edit the gradient. I selected colors that were darker than the sky but brighter than the church. That way they would only appear where the colors applied were brighter than the image, which would cause them to only affect the church. I allowed the orange color on the right of the gradient (which is darker than the sky) to extend quite a distance toward the left, which would usually cause the color to fill the brighter areas of the image (the sky). Since the adjustment was done in the Lighter Color mode, the orange color did not affect the sky because it would have darkened it, which isn't possible when using Lighter Color mode.

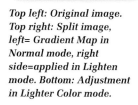

Top left: Original image. Top right: Split image, left= Gradient Map in Normal mode, right side=applied in Lighten mode. Bottom: Adjustment in Lighter Color mode.

The next two features work hand-in-hand to help you produce higher quality panorama images and to better composite multiple shots in general. Personally, I think these are the true stars of the show when it comes to the Photoshop CS3 upgrade. I'm absolutely amazed at how much of an improvement they've made by implementing these two deceptively simple commands.

Auto-Align Layers

The new **Auto-Align Layers** command (which is found in the **Edit** menu) will attempt to align common content in the layers that are selected. There are four options related to this command and we'll explore them one at a time:

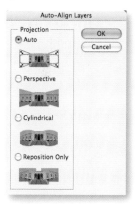

You'll be presented with the following options when you choose Edit>Auto-Align Layers.

Auto: Will analyze the selected layers and attempt to determine the best alignment method automatically. Most of the time it does a pretty good job of figuring out the best alternative, but don't be afraid to try the other options if it doesn't produce great results.

Perspective: Will align the selected layers by adjusting the position of the four corners of each layer and produce a trapezoid out of each layer.

Cylindrical: Will not only adjust the corners of each layer, but will also bend the sides of the layer (and therefore the content inside) so that they are curved.

Reposition Only: Can only change the position of a layer and cannot scale or rotate it in any way.

With all of these methods, Photoshop will increase the canvas size to accommodate the newly positioned content.

In the example below, I started with two images: One had an acceptable body position but the head didn't look good. In the second image, the head was positioned nicely, but the arms and hands of the model were not in a desirable position. Since both shots were taken hand-held, the backgrounds of the two images did not match up when I dragged the two images into a single document.

Right: Result of combining two original images.

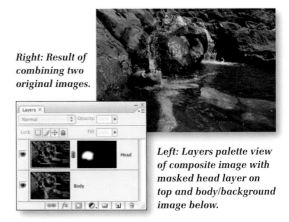

Left: Layers palette view of composite image with masked head layer on top and body/background image below.

To make for an easier compositing job, I selected both layers and chose **Edit>Auto-Align Layers**, which caused the backgrounds in both images to match rather closely. I then added a Layer Mask to the top layer and painted with black to hide all except the model's head. Had I not aligned the two images, painting on the mask would have caused the misalignment to be apparent.

You can see how closely two layers align by changing the Blending Mode menu at the top of the Layers palette to Difference mode. That will cause areas that align perfectly to appear as solid black and areas that don't match up to appear as brighter shades. In this case, the water and model change position in each shot, so those areas appear in color while most of the background appears as solid black after aligning the layers.

Right: Original with good body position, but undesirable head position.

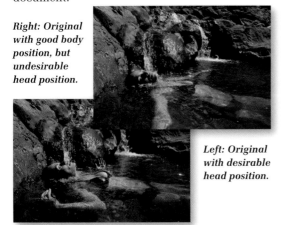

Left: Original with desirable head position.

Alignment comparison: Left=Original, Bottom= Result of Auto-Align.

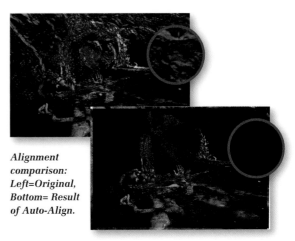

Auto-Blend Layers

The new **Auto-Blend Layers** command (found under the **Edit** menu) was designed to be applied after closely aligning layers either manually or using the new **Auto-Align Layers** command. When you apply the **Auto-Blend Layers** command, it will analyze the selected layers and attempt to match the brightness, color and position of each layer by adjusting the layer and masking the results.

This command is only capable of performing slight changes to the position of the selected layers, but will often match up seams that were still visible after applying the **Auto-Align Layers** command. It really does a spectacular job of matching the color and brightness of images, and it's a hoot to just sit back and watch it perform its magic.

The result of applying the Auto-Blend Layers command on images that were first aligned with the different Auto-Align Layers options.

I find that I can often get away with using images that were shot in automatic mode—where the exposure varies wildly between shots—and it can still smooth them out. In fact, I've started to make radical panorama images by leaving the camera on auto-exposure and using the rapid shooting mode to capture a scene as a series of overlapping images, shot much like you might use a machine gun to spray a scene with bullets. The example to the left shows a scene I photographed using this technique. It involves over 170 shots that were taken in about a five minute time span. I started by using the **Auto-Align Layers** command to align all the images that were shot. I then turned off the eyeball icon for each layer that I felt did not contribute to the end result I was looking for. Those were mainly shots that were overexposed and overlapped properly exposed shots. To finish the panorama, I selected all the visible layers and applied the **Auto-Blend Layers** command.

Load Files Into Stack Script

When a panorama consists of a large number of images it becomes impractical to manually drag all the images into a single file. Adobe has included a new script in Photoshop CS3 that can automatically combine multiple images into a single document. Choosing **File>Scripts>Load Files into Stack** will cause a dialog box to appear asking you to specify which images you'd like to combine into a single document. You can either click the Browse button to navigate your hard drive and point Photoshop to the images you'd like to use, or use the Add Open Files button to have Photoshop combine the files that are currently open. Turning on the **Attempt to Automatically Align Source Image** checkbox will cause it to apply the **Auto-Align Layers** command (using the Auto setting) immediately after combining the images into a single file.

The Load Files into Stack dialog box.

Five images used to produce the panorama photos shown on the next page.

Top to bottom: Perspective, Cylindrical, Reposition Only, Interactive Layout Photomerge results without Auto-Blending.

Top to bottom: Perspective, Cylindrical, Reposition Only, Interactive Layout Photomerge results with Auto-Blending.

Top: Auto merged before blending. Bottom: Result of hiding images that were too bright and Auto-Blending applied.

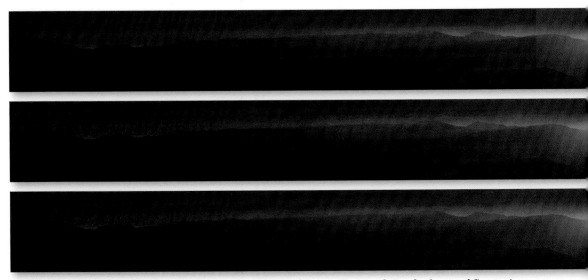

Top to bottom: Manually aligned, result of applying Auto-Blend Layers Command, Result of manual fine-tuning.

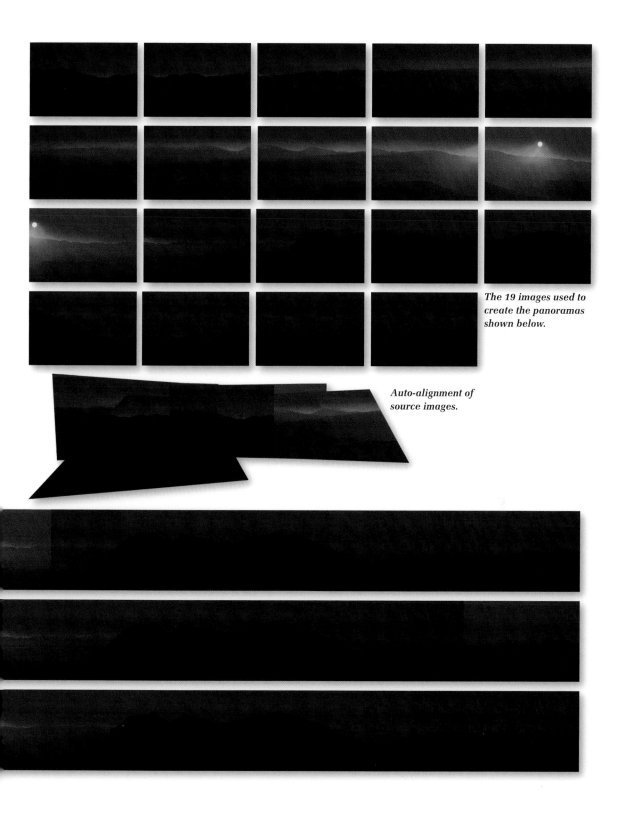

The 19 images used to
create the panoramas
shown below.

Auto-alignment of
source images.

Photomerge

The **Photomerge** command, which is found under the **File>Automate** menu in Photoshop and the **Tools>Photoshop** menu in Bridge, simply combines the **Load Files into Stack** command with the **Auto-Align Layers** command. You can also have Photoshop automatically apply the **Auto-Blend Layers** command by turning on the **Blend images together** checkbox in the Photomerge dialog box.

The Photomerge dialog box offers one alignment choice that is not available when aligning images via the **Edit>Auto-Align Layers** command. The **Interactive Layout** choice will present you with the Photomerge choices that were available in previous versions of Photoshop. I rarely use the Interactive Layout feature since its automatic alignment ability feels like stone-age technology when compared to the new offerings in Photoshop CS3.

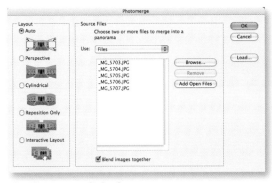

The Photomerge dialog box.

I often prefer to use the individual commands to combine, align and blend layers instead of the Photomerge command because I find I like to fine-tune the results of each stage of the process to either manually align images that the automated technique didn't properly align (which is very common on 360° panoramas), or hide layers that contain images that are not properly exposed.

It was such a pleasure working with the new features in this chapter. I hope you'll get the same sense of wonder that I did when playing with the new toys. For the photography crowd, the Auto-Blend/Auto-Align tools should save you enough time to extend your next shooting safari by an extra day! For you design folks, the new Smart Filters and all of their attached bells and whistles should have an equally dramatic effect, not only saving you untold hours, but giving you the opportunity to experiment freely without the agony of having to start over again if you didn't like the result of a particular filter. This all means more time for the good stuff in life, and less time hunched over our computers. As Martha Stewart would say, "That's a good thing."

Chapter 7
General Improvements

THIS CHAPTER IS HOME FOR all those new or revamped features that don't easily fit into big broad categories. It doesn't mean they are not significant or important to the way you'll work in Photoshop, it just means that together they are a bit of a mish-mash, albeit a savory one with some tasty bits you won't want to miss.

Below is an overview of what we'll be covering in this chapter:

- **Device Central:** Create images sized for cell phones and other mobile devices, and then preview them in a nifty new emulator.
- **Vanishing Point:** Make your images or retouching wrap around corners, giving your images a striking 3D impression.
- **Printing:** Explore the reorganized Print dialog box and discover some very welcome features, including one which actually puts meaning back into the words, "Print Preview."
- **Preferences:** Learn about all of the changes made to the Preferences dialog box (there were a boat load), including one that will help you better manage Photoshop's memory usage.
- **Misc. Changes:** Find out what you need to know about all the tiny tweaks that you might miss if you aren't looking close enough.
- **Extended Features:** Get a peek at one Extended feature (Image Stacks) that could be of great interest to you if you're a graphic designer or photographer.

Where's My Stuff?

Let's look at what's happened to some of the features you might have used in previous versions of Photoshop:

- **ImageReady:** Adobe ImageReady (the web graphics application that was bundled with Photoshop) has been discontinued. Over the last few years, Adobe migrated many of its features into Photoshop, but with the loss of the full version, you can no longer create rollovers and image maps. If this functionality is important to you, you'll need to keep a copy of ImageReady CS2 installed, or move to another product like Adobe Fireworks.
- **Welcome Screen:** The splash screen that appeared the first time you launched Photoshop—it was also accessible from the **Help>Welcome Screen** menu— has been removed. There is no replacement for it, but don't let that make you feel unwelcome.
- **Export Transparent Image:** This feature has been removed from the **Help** menu and there is no replacement for it.

- **Resize Image:** Adobe removed this command from the **Help** menu so you'll now have to manually resize your images.
- **Transfer Activation:** The **Transfer Activation** command in the **Help** menu has simply been renamed **Deactivate**.
- **Print with Preview:** The **Print with Preview** dialog box has been replaced with a new print dialog box that we'll discuss in this chapter.
- **Zoom View:** The **Zoom View** command that was found under the **File>Export** menu has been replaced with the new **Zoomify** command, which is found in the same menu.
- **Preference Settings:** Many of Photoshop's Preference settings have been moved around within the Preferences dialog box. There are quite a few changes, all of which will be described in the Preferences section of this chapter.
- **Vanishing Point:** If you're used to holding **Option** (Mac), or **Alt** (Win) when clicking the **OK** button to have Photoshop render the grid onto your image, you'll now have to choose the **Render Grid** option from the side menu within Vanishing Point (see the Vanishing Point section for more detail).

Now that we've got our bearings, let's dive right in to the new features, starting with one that is all about keeping up with our high-tech times.

Device Central

Adobe Device Central is a new application that is included with Photoshop CS3. It is designed to make it easier to create content that is destined to appear on a mobile device like a cellular telephone. Let's take a look at some of the basic features of this new application.

New Document for Device
The first step for creating mobile content is to create a new document that is the proper size for the device on which the image will be viewed. To do this, you'll need to open Device Central by either choosing **Edit>Device Central**, or clicking the **Device Central** button that is found in the **File>New** dialog box. You'll find a list of various

Choose from the Content Type pop-up menu before clicking the Create button to create a new document.

cell phone models along the left side of the dialog box. Clicking on the name of a device will display a photo of the model along with its specifications under the **Device Profiles** tab. To create a document, click on the **New Document** tab and choose from the **Content Type** pop-up menu to specify how the image will be used (Fullscreen, Screen Saver, etc.) and click on the **Create** button. Photoshop will produce an empty document of the appropriate size for your chosen device.

Not Using Photoshop?
You can also create a new document in another program (such as Adobe Illustrator or Adobe Flash) by choosing from the File>New Document In menu.

If you don't find the mobile device you desire from the list, choose **Check for Device Updates** from the **Devices** menu in Device Central to see if Adobe has released a new profile for the device.

Test Content on Simulated Device
Once you are done creating the imagery you plan to display, choose **File>Save for Web & Devices**, specify your desired file format options and click the **Device Central** button found near the bottom right of the Save for Web & Devices

Pre-existing Content
If you'd like to test content that you've already saved, select the image in Bridge and choose File>Test in Device Central from within Bridge.

Clicking on the name of a device from the list on the left will cause Device Central to display the specifications for the chosen model under the Content tab.

dialog box. That will cause Device Central to appear again, but this time it will be in Emulator mode, which allows you to preview how your image might look on your chosen device. There are all sorts of options available in the emulator (such as the ability to simulate reflections on the screen), and they are all easy to use.

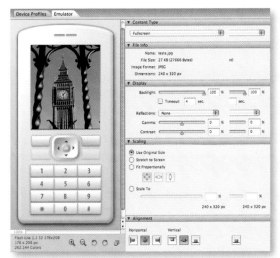

Choosing Device Central from within the Save for Web & Devices dialog box will cause Device Central to preview how the image might look on a mobile device.

Saving the Image

None of the controls found in the Device Central dialog box will allow you to actually save your image. You'll have to return to Photoshop's Save for Web & Devices dialog box (choose **File>Return to Photoshop**) and click the **Save** button to save your image.

For more information about using Device Central and developing content for mobile devices, choose **Device Central Online** from the **Help** menu within Device Central. That will launch your web browser and bring you to a special section of Adobe's web site where you'll find an extensive amount of content related to developing content for mobile devices.

> ### NOTE
>
> **Designed for Flash**
> *Adobe Device Central was developed to make it easier to develop and test Adobe Flash content that will be used on a mobile device. I won't describe all the features in Device Central because I believe it is of limited benefit to people who strictly use Photoshop and it better serves those who develop Flash content outside of Photoshop.*

Vanishing Point

When you first choose **Filter>Vanishing Point**, you might not notice any significant changes, but if you give it some time, you'll find a few gems that are worth exploring. Let's start with the tiny enhancements and then progress into the more important ones.

For starters, Adobe has revised a few of the icons that appear in the upper left of the Vanishing Point dialog box. These changes are purely cosmetic and do not affect the way you work with the tools represented by the icons.

Left: The Edit Plane (top) and Create Plane tools (bottom) as they appeared in Photoshop CS2. Right: The Photoshop CS3 version of the same tools.

A few features have been moved. The **Show Edges** checkbox that was found in CS2 has been transformed into the **Show Edges** option that is found in the side menu near the top left of the dialog box. The ability to have the plane grids overlaid onto your image has been moved to the same side menu (in CS2, you had to hold **Option** or **Alt** when pressing the **OK** button to access this feature).

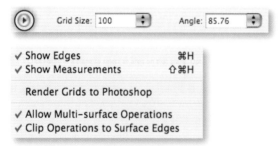

Top: Options for Edit Plane tool.
Bottom: Options found in side menu.

Connected Planes

In Photoshop CS2, after you had defined one plane with the **Create Plane** tool, you could hold **Command** (Mac), or **Ctrl** (Win) and drag one of the side handles of the plane with the **Edit Plane** tool to create a second plane that was connected at a 90 degree angle to the first plane (as if they were joined together by a hinge). This was useful when working with buildings since walls are most commonly built at 90 degree angles to one another.

In CS3, Adobe added the capability to create connected planes that can be at any angle relative to each other. After creating a 90 degree plane as described above, hold **Option** (Mac), or **Alt** (Win) and drag the side handle that is opposite the hinge (connecting the two planes) to change the angle of one plane relative to the other. Changing the angle of a connected plane is just like opening or closing the cover of a book. When you do that, you are essentially changing the angle of two rectangular surfaces (or planes) that are connected together with a hinge-like binding.

In Photoshop CS2, Vanishing Point's tools treated each plane as an isolated area that was completely independent from all the other planes you had defined (almost like a separate document)—no operation could span more than one plane. That's all changed in Photoshop CS3's Vanishing Point dialog box.

> **NOTE**
>
> **Precise Angles**
> You can also change the angle of a connected plane by adjusting the **Angle** setting that is found at the top of the Vanishing Point dialog box. I often click on a connected plane with the **Edit Plane** tool to make it active, click on the **Angle** setting and then use the **Up Arrow** and **Down Arrow** keys to adjust the Angle setting.

First plane defined by clicking on the four corners of a rectangular surface using the Create Plane tool.

Second plane defined at 90 degrees from first plane by Command/Ctrl-dragging the side handle of the first plane.

Result of Option/Alt dragging the side handle of the second plane to change its angle relative to the first plane.

A portion of this image was copied and pasted into Vanishing Point in the example shown on the next page.

This image offered multiple 90 degree angles that were easy to define in Vanishing Point.

Multi-Surface Operations

In CS3, the **Allow Multi-surface Operations** option that is found in the side menu near the top of the Vanishing Point dialog box (it's on by default) will cause all connected planes to be treated as a single continuous surface. That means you can now paint, apply retouching, or copy/paste an image so that it extends across one or more connected planes.

My favorite use for this new feature is to copy and paste an image into Vanishing Point and have it bend around a corner. You could also use this new feature to place a floor rug down a set of stairs and have it bend to conform to the surface of each stair.

Allow Multi-Surface Operations

To cause an image to span multiple planes, do the following: **1)** Open the image you'd like to place, make a selection of the area you'd like to use, choose **Edit>Copy. 2)** Choose **Filter>Vanishing Point**, define at least one connected plane and double-check that the **Allow Multi-surface Operations** option is turned on. **3)** Type **Command-V** (Mac), or **Ctrl-V** (Win) to paste the image into Vanishing Point (you must use this keyboard shortcut since **Paste** is not available from the **Edit** menu when working in Vanishing Point) and then drag the image onto one of the two connected planes.

Turning off the **Allow Multi-surface Operations** option will cause Vanishing Point to treat each plane independently of each other, which will prevent all tools from treating two planes as a continuous surface.

Clip Operations to Surface Edges

With default settings, Photoshop will constrain all pasted images so that they do not extend beyond the bounds of the plane on which you drag the image. If you'd rather allow the image to extend beyond the bounds of the planes (the way it always worked in CS2), turn off the **Clip Operations to Surface Edges** option in the side menu that's found near the top of the Vanishing Point dialog box (this option is turned on by default).

Result of copy/pasting an image into Vanishing Point and placing it onto two connected planes.

Result of turning off the All Multi-Surface Operations option from the side menu in Vanishing Point.

Result of turning off the Clip Operations to Surface Edged option from the side menu in Vanishing Point.

Printing

The Print with Preview dialog box has been replaced by a redesigned print dialog box that can be found by choosing **File>Print**. The main complaint about the old version was that despite its name, it didn't actually feature an accurate preview. It only previewed the size of the image compared to the size of the paper on which you were printing and did not display an accurate preview of how the colors within your image would print. CS3 has come to the rescue with some great new features that make previewing much easier and more accurate.

NOTE

Preview Accuracy

Many printers can produce colors that are beyond the range that can be displayed on-screen (like vivid yellows) and most monitors can display colors that are beyond the range that can be reproduced on a printer (like vivid blues). If the Match Print Colors feature does not provide a good match between your monitor and printer, you're either running into the limitations of your monitor or the monitor and/or printer profiles being used are not accurate enough to produce an acceptable preview.

Match Print Colors

Turning on the new Match Print Colors checkbox will cause Photoshop to attempt to simulate how your image will look when printed using the printer profile you've specified in the Color Management section of the dialog box. This option will only be available when the **Color Handling** pop-up menu is set to **Photoshop Manages Colors**. That's because Photoshop cannot determine what your image would look like if you use your printer driver to manage the colors when printing (which are specified after you leave the Print dialog box).

Other Changes

The new **Printer** pop-up menu allows you to select the printer you will be using, and will inform Photoshop of the media size limitations of that particular device.

A new **Print Resolution** readout has been added that reflects the effective resolution of your image after it has been scaled according to the settings you've specified. That's a nice addition because it helps you to avoid scaling the image so large that you'd see pixelation. Going below 150PPI has the potential to produce jaggy edges on angled lines.

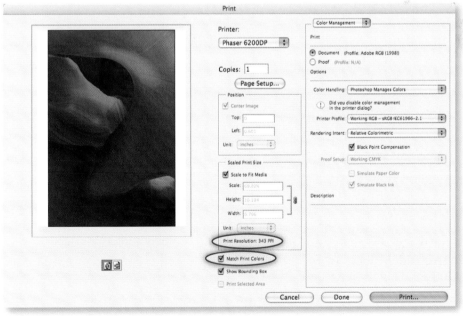

The new Print dialog box in Photoshop CS3.

Preferences

Adobe has reorganized the Preferences dialog box by shuffling the settings that were previously organized in nine categories into a new group of ten categories. They are listed down the left side of the Preferences dialog box instead of being shown in a menu as in the previous version.

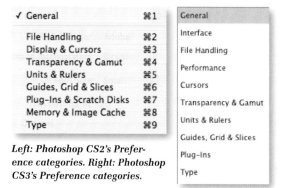

Left: Photoshop CS2's Preference categories. Right: Photoshop CS3's Preference categories.

Let's take a stroll through each of the new categories and see what's been moved, renamed and added in Photoshop CS3.

General Preferences: The **Show Tool Tips** checkbox has been moved to the new Interface section of the Preferences dialog box along with the **Show Menu Colors** checkbox. The old **Save Palette Locations** checkbox has been renamed **Remember Palette Locations** and was also moved

to the Interface section of the dialog box. The History States setting (which determines how many undos are available in Photoshop) has also been moved, this time to the Performance section since keeping track of more history states can consume a lot of hard drive space, which could sacrifice performance.

Interface Preferences: This new section contains many of the settings that were previously found in the General and Displays & Cursors sections in Photoshop CS2 along with two new options: The new **Use Grayscale Toolbar Icon** checkbox will cause the blue "PS" that appears at the top of the Toolbar to become gray, which is desirable when you don't want Photoshop's user interface to distract from the colors used within your images. The new **Auto-Collapse Icon Palettes** checkbox will cause palettes that have been expanded from an icon to collapse when you click outside of the palette (as described in the Interface Changes chapter).

The new Interface section of the Preferences dialog box.

Photoshop CS3s Preferences dialog box.

File Handling Preferences: The **Enable Large Document Format (.psb)** checkbox that was found in Photoshop CS2 has been removed because Adobe decided to no longer allow you to disable the feature. The **Prefer Adobe Camera Raw for JPEG files** and **Prefer Adobe Camera Raw for Supported Raw Files** are new additions that were discussed in the Bridge and Camera Raw chapters of this book.

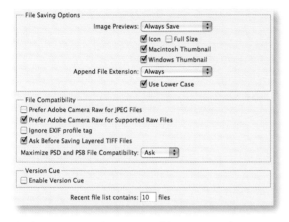

Performance Preferences: This new section contains many of the settings that were previously found in the Memory & Image Cache and Plug-Ins & Scratch Disks sections in Photoshop CS2 along with the **History States** setting that used to be found in the General section.

The Memory Usage setting now indicates what Adobe feels is the ideal range for how much memory Photoshop should be able to access. You can adjust the setting by entering a number, dragging a slider, or clicking the **plus** and **minus** buttons.

The Scratch Disks section now indicates how much free space is available on each hard drive, making it easier to determine which drive has enough open space to be effectively used as a scratch disk.

The **Pixel Doubling** feature that was previously found in the Displays & Cursors section in CS2 didn't make it to CS3. That feature was designed to speed up the screen redraw when moving a layer on low end computers. I think Adobe removed it for two reasons: **1)** The computers available today are much faster than the ones that were around when that feature was introduced and **2)** Almost no one knew what that feature was for and therefore very few people would care if it were removed.

Transparency & Gamut Preferences: The only change that was made here was to remove the **Use Video Alpha** checkbox. That feature was necessary when outputting images to video using hardware that is now completely outdated. It made sense to get rid of it because people who are working with such ancient hardware are not likely to be operating this version of Photoshop.

Now that you've seen all the changes that have happened in the Preferences dialog box, let's start to explore more of the nooks and crannies of Photoshop to see what small features Adobe snuck into this upgrade.

Misc. Changes

This next bunch of tweaks are not immediately obvious, but many are worth knowing about.

Updated for New OS's: Photoshop CS3 is now a Universal Binary application on the Macintosh, which means that it will run much faster on Intel-based Macs when compared to CS2. Adobe also did some work to make Photoshop compatible with Windows Vista.

Faster Launch: Photoshop has been optimized so that it launches at least 20% faster than previous versions.

Interpolation Hints: Adobe added additional text to the choices found under the Interpolation menu in the Image Size dialog box to make it easier to figure out which setting is most ideal for your situation. The menu choices produce the exact same results as CS2, but now each setting comes with a little explanation of why you might use it.

> Nearest Neighbor (preserve hard edges)
> Bilinear
> ✓ Bicubic (best for smooth gradients)
> Bicubic Smoother (best for enlargement)
> Bicubic Sharper (best for reduction)

Swatches from Color Picker: An **Add to Swatches** button is now available in the color picker so you can add the current foreground color to the Swatches palette directly from the Color Picker dialog box.

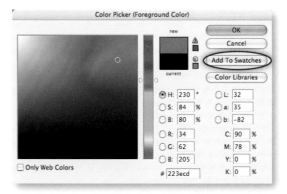

Save for Web & Devices: Save for Web has become **Save for Web & Devices** because it is also commonly used to save images that are destined for mobile devices like cellular telephones. Adobe also added a very welcome **Convert to sRGB** choice in the side menu that is found to the right of the **Preset** pop-up menu. Having this setting turned on will cause Photoshop to apply the **Convert to Profile** command that is found under the **Edit** menu and will convert the image to the sRGB color space. That will cause the image to more closely match what it looked like in Photoshop when you view the image in a web browser or other application that does not fully support color management. I've been begging Adobe to implement this change for years and am thrilled to see its arrival in CS3.

PDF Presentation: You can now choose to show different types of metadata (Filename, Copyright, etc.) below each image in a PDF presentation. This is useful when you need to get feedback from a client and don't want to hear vague things like "use the blue-ish image." If a client can see the file names of an image, there is a chance that he or she will provide more useful feedback.

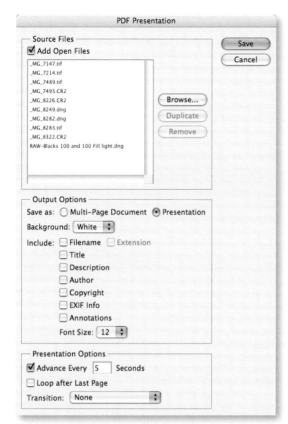

Photoshop CS3's PDF Presentation dialog box is accessed by choosing File>Automate>PDF Presentation.

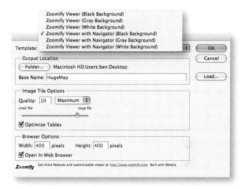

Zoomify: This is a great new feature that will make life easier for all those folks who need to place large images on a web page so that visitors can zoom in and pan around to see all the fine details. This is done by utilizing the same technology that's used to view maps at www.maps.google.com. Choosing **File>Export>Zoomify** will present you with a dialog box full of options.

At the top you specify the type of interface you'd like to use to navigate your image and which color you'd like to see fill the rest of the browser window. Below that you specify the folder to which you'd like to save the image and the quality settings you'd like to use (just like when saving a JPEG file). At the bottom you can specify how much of the area the image will take up when viewed in a web browser. When you click the OK button, Photoshop will create an HTML file and a folder that contains the image components in the location you've specified.

When you open the HTML file in a web browser, you'll be presented with an interface that allows you to browse your image. You can zoom in or out on the image by dragging the slider that appears at the bottom of the image, or holding **Shift** to zoom in and **Command** (Mac), or **Ctrl** (Win) to zoom out.

Photoshop CS2's PDF Presentation dialog box.

Scripting: Let's look at scripting in two sections: **1)** The changes they've made to the scripts that come with Photoshop. **2)** Changes they've made that add functionality for those people who create their own scripts.

Changes to Existing Scripts

The **Image Processor** that can be found under the **File>Scripts** menu in Photoshop and the **Tools>Photoshop** menu in Bridge is a script that allows you to quickly scale and save multiple images. Adobe changed the script so that any action that is to be applied (via the menu at the bottom of the Image Processor dialog box) will be applied after the image has been scaled instead of before (as it was in previous versions).

A new script was added to the **File>Scripts** menu that's called **Load Files into Stack**. This script allows you to feed Photoshop a list of files (via the **Browse** or **Add Open Files** buttons) and have it combine all the images into a single document where each image becomes a separate layer.

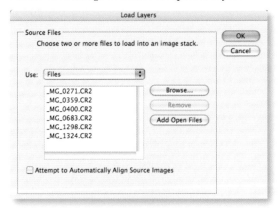

Using the Load Files into Stack Script

Let's look at a situation where I found this feature to be especially useful. In the example below I wanted to remove the mist that was coming off a waterfall. To accomplish that, I shot over a dozen photographs of the waterfall while my camera was on a tripod (I noticed that the mist was in a different position in each shot).

I used the Load Files into Stack script to combine all the images into a single Photoshop file. I then changed the blending mode menu at the top of the Layers palette to Darken on each of the layers so that Photoshop would compare them all and only use the darkest areas of each shot. That caused the breaks in the mist to be used (because they were darker than the areas that contained mist in the other shots), which effectively removed the mist.

After removing the mist, I noticed that a lot of the white areas in the waterfall had also been removed. To get the waterfall back to its original look, I placed all but the bottom layer into a Group (which looks like a folder in the Layers palette), added a Layer Mask to the Group and then painted with black to remove the effect of the layers from the waterfall area.

New Features for Creating Scripts

Now let's shift gears and look at what's new for people who create their own scripts. Casual users who have never created a script should definitely skip this section and start reading again when you get to the next heading, Extended Features.

Adobe has done considerable work to the underpinnings that allow Photoshop to be scriptable. Among other things, they've added XML parsing support and there's a new version of the ExtendScript Toolkit that can be useful when creating your own scripts. You can also now call one script from within another, which was not possible in CS2.

> **NOTE**
>
> **Creating Scripts**
> Creating scripts is really beyond the scope of this book—because it's related to programming and that's not usually the domain of graphic designers and photographers who are the main audience for this book. For that reason, I will only present a brief summary of the changes related to creating scripts.

Finally, Adobe embedded the Adobe Flash player into Photoshop which will allow Flash developers to create products that incorporate interface elements and video that are used from within Photoshop.

At this point we've covered all of the important new features in Photoshop CS3 standard edition. Now let's look at one feature from the Extended version of CS3 that I'm amazed Adobe didn't include in the standard version (Adobe Photoshop CS3 Extended includes all the features of regular Photoshop CS3, plus more.)

Just a reminder: the majority of Extended features are mainly of interest to scientists, medical professionals and people who work with video and 3D. This book is intended for photographers and graphic designers (which is my area of expertise), so with the exception of Image Stacks, which I think could be very interesting to regular users, the majority of Extended features are beyond the scope of this book and are not covered in any kind of detail.

Extended Features

The Image Stacks feature in CS3 Extended was designed for scientists who needed to have Photoshop compare or perform calculations on multiple images that contain similar content (like comparing multiple MRI images to see if a patient's brain tumor continues to grow over time). It makes perfect sense that this feature should be included in the Extended version of Photoshop because the extra features in that version are primarily designed for scientific imaging.

What Adobe didn't realize was that the Image Stacks feature has a few uses that make it appropriate for all users of Photoshop. Let's take a look at how to use the Image Stacks feature and then explore ways in which photographers and graphic designers could use it to great benefit.

Image Stacks

The first thing you need to do is to combine multiple images into a single, layered Photoshop file. Once all the images you'd like to use appear as separate layers, you'll need to select those layers and choose **Layers> Smart Objects>Convert to Smart Object** so that Photoshop knows they should all relate to each other. Finally, you can have Photoshop analyze the layers by choosing from the options that are found under the **Layers>Smart Objects>Stack Mode** menu.

> **NOTE**
>
> **Automated Stacks**
> You can create an Image Stack in a single step by using the *File>Scripts>Load Files into Stack* script that was mentioned a few pages back. An extra checkbox called **Create Smart Object After Loading Layers** will appear in the Load Files into Stack dialog box when you have the Extended version of Photoshop installed.

Most of the choices available in that menu will produce unusual results and are mainly useful for scientific analysis of images. There is one mode, however, that could be of use to everyone and it's called **Median**. It will compare all the layers in a stack and keep whatever is the most consistent between all the layers. Following are a couple of examples which show you how awesome this feature can be when put to work.

Left: A single shot taken at ISO 3200 produces a significant amount of noise.

Right: Six ISO 3200 shots combined using Median mode produces an image with a lot less noise.

From Left to Right: Number of shots being combined in Median mode (with some contrast enhancement to make it easier to see the noise)—Single shot, 2 shots, 3 shots, 4 shots, 5 shots, 6 shots.

Reducing Noise

The image above was taken using a high ISO setting on a digital camera (also known as film speed) which produced a very noisy image. Because noise is random, taking six shots of the scene produced six images that contained slightly different noise patterns. Combining those six images using Median mode dramatically reduced the amount of noise in the image as the noise was not consistent between the images.

Eliminating Objects

In the image below, I was photographing a sunset but was unhappy that the animals in the shot were always clustered together. I noticed that one animal was remaining stationary, so I took three shots and combined them using Median mode. That caused Photoshop to only keep the areas that were consistent between all the shots, which had the effect of removing the bothersome animals that changed position between the shots.

Left: Three images that were used within a stack. Right: The result of combining the images using Median mode.

Keep in Touch

Anyone who has been around Photoshop for more than two minutes knows that this is an application with a daunting arsenal of tools. CS3 added another level of power and complexity, making the learning curve a few inches longer. Many features are relatively straightforward and easy to grasp, while others can present a bit of an obstacle course. Sometimes the biggest challenge is simply knowing which tool to use! That's why learning Photoshop is a life-long pursuit for anyone serious about mastering its full potential.

Books are essential ingredients in the stew of resources necessary to keep us functioning as Photoshop superheroes, but there is an entire universe of other resources out there that will do wonders to support your personal evolution with digital imaging. My part of that universe is available through my web site, DigitalMastery.com, and my blog, WhereisBen.com.

At **DigitalMastery.com** you'll find my seminar/conference schedule, books and DVDs, as well a bunch of free resources including my magazine articles, tips and tutorials.

At **WhereisBen.com** you'll find my travel diary (destinations range from Dubai, Russia, and Iceland to places as obscure as Kerrville, Texas), my latest photos, more magazine articles, radio interviews, favorite web sites and gadgets, and just about anything I find interesting.

I encourage you to visit my sites, and I'd love to see you at one my events, or hear from you if you have something to say that you feel would make this a better book. Just write to me at book@digitalmastery.com, or throw something (preferably soft) at me when you see me at PhotoshopWorld or at one of my seminars to get my attention.

Best of luck to you as you wrap yourself around CS3. I hope this book gives you what you need as you launch yourself toward Photoshop nirvana!

Bonus Chapter

Still Learning CS2?

If you're like most folks with busy lives and endless deadlines, you probably just cherry-pick features out of each Photoshop upgrade and think to yourself that you'll catch up with the rest of the upgrade later. And if you're like most, you find that by the time "later" rolls around, Adobe has released yet another Photoshop upgrade, and now you've got that many more new features to absorb!

If that describes you, and you found this book to be useful, imagine how the CS2 version of this book could help you master all those features that you didn't get to or aren't using to their fullest extent.

Up to Speed: Adobe Photoshop CS2 provides in-depth coverage of every new feature in the CS2 upgrade including full chapters dedicated to Variables, Smart Objects, the revised Layers Palette and HDR imaging (all features that haven't changed in CS3).

The following Bonus chapter is from that book and covers a wonderful feature called Variables. Variables is not for everyone and might not do much for you if you don't work with large quantities of diverse output, but if you are someone who works with large-scale projects that involve some degree of variation—product packaging, awards, invitations, business cards, multi-language output, for example—this feature is a veritable gold mine!

Enjoy the bonus chapter, and know that you can always look for an Up to Speed book whenever you hear a new version of Photoshop is on the way.

Up to Speed: Adobe Photoshop CS2
By Ben Willmore
Published by Peachpit Press
ISBN-10: 0-321-33050-1

To purchase this book, go to **DigitalMastery.com**, or any major bookseller.

"Hands-down, this is simply the best book for 'getting up to speed' with Photoshop CS2. Adobe should include it with every copy of Photoshop."
—Chris Murphy, Co-Author, *Real World Color Management* (ColorRemedies.com)

"Ben's book gets to the heart of Photoshop CS2 - what has changed, what is new, and how you can get the most out of the features as quickly as possible. With 'Up to Speed' you will be taking advantage of Photoshop CS2 in no time at all.
—Katrin Eismann Author, *Photoshop Retouching & Restoration* (PhotoshopDiva.com)

Swan
Maria Gonzales
(303) 555-1919 • maria@swansoap.com
63 Lilypad Drive • Clear Lake, CO 88129
www.swansoap.com

Swan
Lucy Woo
555-1818 • lucy@swansoap.com
63 Lilypad Drive • Clear Lake, CO 88129
www.swansoap.com

Swan
Bennie Smith
555-1717 • bennie@swansoap.com
63 Lilypad Drive • Clear Lake, CO 88129
www.swansoap.com

Bonus Chapter
Variables

I IF YOU FIND YOURSELF NEEDING to create dozens or even hundreds of documents that have a common underlying design, and in which the only variables are the text and graphic elements (business cards, invites, packaging or awards, for example), then you'll go nuts for Photoshop's new Variables feature, which can only be called a miracle of automation.

Variables allows you to create templates that contain placeholder text and graphics. The placeholder elements can be quickly switched out with the contents of a simple text file that lists the text and graphics you wish to use for alternate versions of the document. This enables you to automatically produce multiple graphic files that are variations on the template design. Still not with me? Here's an extreme example of how this feature could save you days of work.

Imagine that you're the sole designer for a large corporate behemoth. The muckety-mucks on the top floor order a complete redesign of the corporate identity. Excited at the opportunity, you labor away creating fresh designs for business cards, letterhead and envelopes. After having your design approved, you're given the task of preparing press-ready files for all 20,000 employees! Knowing how to use Variables, you request a text file that lists all employee names and other vital information. You feed the file to Photoshop and leave on a three day vacation as Photoshop processes the data and automatically creates no less than 60,000 graphic files!

Here's an overview of what's involved when working with Variables:

- **Create Template** to define the overall design of your document.
- **Define Variables** to determine which layers should change between the individual documents.
- **Create Data Sets** to control which images and text should be used for each document you'd like generated.
- **Preview Results** to make sure everything is working as expected.
- **Generate Graphics** by having Photoshop automatically produce separate graphic files for each entry in the Data Set used.

Variables have been a part of ImageReady since the version that shipped with Photoshop 7, so it isn't exactly a new feature, but it is new to Photoshop. Photoshop users who don't bother with ImageReady may be delighted to discover what they've been missing.

A Brief Overview of Variables

To produce multiple graphic files that have a common underlying structure:

1) Create a template file that contains placeholder text and graphics (like a business card that contains a fake name, address, phone number and e-mail address) and defines the general look of the finished files you desire (fonts, colors, size, position of graphic elements, etc.).

2) Make the placeholder layers changeable by assigning each one a unique name (this is how you define them as Variables). The unique names should reflect the purpose of each layer (for the business card example, you might call them 'name,' 'address,' 'phone,' and e-mail').

3) Create a specially formatted text file that lists all the Variables (the unique names mentioned above) and the text and graphics (file names for graphics stored on your hard drive) that should be swapped out for the layers that were used to create the template file (separated by commas). This text file can only contain plain text (no formatting instructions like font size or color) since the style that will be used is defined by the template file. The contents of these text files are rather simple: The first line simply tells Photoshop the order in which the content will be presented by listing the unique names that were assigned to each layer ("name, address, phone, e-mail" for example). All subsequent lines list the content that should populate those layers ("Ben Willmore, 7157 Magnolia Drive, 555-555-1212, book@digitalmastery.com" for example). Each line that contains content is known as a Data Set.

4) Feed that special text file into Photoshop to have separate graphic files created for each Data Set contained in the text file. There is no practical limit to the number of entries that can be in the text file and therefore no limit to the number of graphic files Photoshop can generate.

name	address	phone	email
Ben Willmore	7157 Magnolia Dr.	303-555-3191	book@digitalmastery.com
Regina Cleveland	63 Longmont Dam Rd.	303-555-1234	regina@digitalmastery.com
Nik Willmore	18 110th St	212-555-1418	nik@e-dot.com
Nate Willmore	12 Main St.	303-555-4467	doesnt@haveone.com

This spreadsheet shows Variable names in the top row and four Data Sets in the rows below.

```
name,address,phone,email
Ben Willmore,7157 Magnolia Dr.,303-555-3191,book@digitalmastery.com
Regina Cleveland,63 Longmont Dam Rd.,303-555-1234,regina@digitalmastery.com
Nik Willmore,18 110th St, 212-555-1418,nik@e-dot.com
Nate Willmore,12 Main St.,303-555-4467,doesnt@haveone.com
```

The same file viewed as a comma-delimited text file ready to be fed to Photoshop.

Template file with four Variables assigned to four different text layers (name, address, phone, e-mail).

One of the four graphic files produced by applying the text file shown above.

Create Template

The first step to implementing Variables is to create a template file. This is just an everyday Photoshop file (**File>New**) that will contain placeholder text and graphics that you'd like to later swap out with other content.

Design Considerations

You'll need to create a separate layer for each item you want to be able to swap out. Using a business card as an example, you'll likely end up with separate layers for Name, Title, Address, E-mail, Telephone Number, Fax Number, and Web Site, as well as one for the company logo (if it needs to vary between cards). Here are some things to keep in mind when creating templates:

Leave extra space so text can vary in length without being truncated or bumping into other graphic elements (just because your sample data is short doesn't mean that the replacement text will be the same length).

Consider graphic orientation by planning for both horizontal and vertical images. Using square placeholder graphics will leave room for replacement graphics regardless of their orientation.

Avoid using the Background for items you want to vary. The Background layer cannot be controlled with a Variable, so whatever is on the Background will be consistent between documents.

When creating a template file, use seperate layers for each item that you want to define as a Variable. The Layers palette shown here is for the example image shown on the previous page.

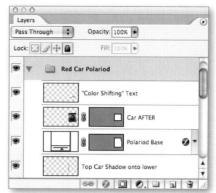

The visibility of the four layers inside this Group can be controlled by a single Variable.

Show/hide multiple layers by placing them into a Group (which looks like a folder and used to be known as a Layer Set). A single Variable can control the visibility of a group and hence all the layers that are contained within the group.

Plan for multiple templates by incorporating all the layers that will be needed collectively for all the templates. If you plan to create multiple template files that will be used with the same data (such as business cards, letterhead and envelopes that all use the same text and graphics), then create a single template document that incorporates all the layers that will be needed for all the templates. For instance, if you start by creating a template for your corporate envelopes (which normally contain just the company logo and address), you'd still want to include layers for information such as e-mail address, phone number and title, even though you don't want them visible on the envelope. Then, after defining the Variables (which we'll talk about in a moment), duplicate the first template and use it as the basis for other templates by simply hiding any layers that you don't want to have visible in each template. That way all the templates can be used with the same data since they all share a common structure of Variables.

Now that you know what's involved with creating templates, it's time to define which layers should vary by assigning Variables to some of the layers that make up the template.

Define Variables

The next step is to tell Photoshop which layers you want to be able to change by defining them as Variables and specifying what should be changeable (contents or visibility). Do this by choosing **Image>Variables>Define**, and select the name of the layer you want to use from the **Layer** pop-up menu (or use the arrows next to the menu to cycle through all the layer names).

Choosing a Variable Type

Once you've found the layer you'd like to define as a Variable, it's time to decide between the three types of Variables that are available:

Visibility

This method allows you to show or hide the contents of a layer. Example: you're designing business cards for a real estate firm where some employees are certified brokers and others are not. The design for everyone's cards will be the identical, but some should display a certification graphic and others should not. Once you've turned on the *Visibility* checkbox, then enter a name that describes the purpose of the layer (such as "certified_logo_visibility").

If your template contains complex multi-layered graphics that you need to show or hide, then place the layers within a Group (which looks like a folder) and define the Group as a Variable.

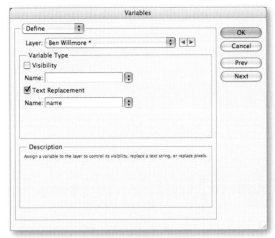

Choose Image>Variables>Define to access this dialog.

Text Replacement

This method allows you to replace a string of text with alternate text from an external file (we'll talk about those text files soon). This type of Variable is essential when creating a series of business cards or other documents that need to be personalized for each employee in a company.

Pixel Replacement

This method replaces the contents of a pixel-based layer with an external image file. Since the size of images can vary widely, Photoshop offers four methods for scaling the imported graphics to fit the space defined by the placeholder image (known as the layer's bounding box):

Fit will scale the graphic until it fits within the bounds of the placeholder image while maintaining the width/height proportions of the replacement graphic file. This is the setting I use for about 90% of the graphics I work with because all the other methods have the potential to crop or distort the images.

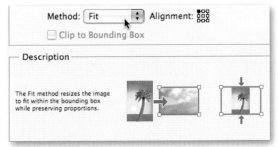

The Fit Method.

Fill will scale the graphic until it completely fills the space taken up by the placeholder image, while still maintaining the width/height proportions of the replacement graphic file. That can cause the replacement graphic to become larger than the placeholder image, which will create layout problems. You can hide the areas of the graphic that extend beyond the placeholder image by turning on the *Clip to Bounding Box* checkbox. I mainly use this setting with organic looking images (water, bark, etc.) or patterns (brick, fabric, etc.) where it's more important to have consistently sized graphics and it doesn't matter how the image ends up being cropped.

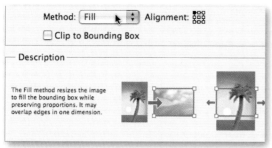

The Fill Method.

As Is will not scale the replacement graphic at all. I only use this setting when it's important to display the image at a specific size (as when demonstrating the exact size of a product). If you'd like to hide any areas that extend beyond the placeholder image, then turn on the *Clip to Bounding Box* checkbox.

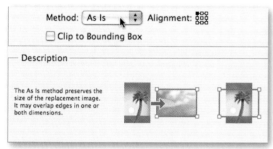

The As Is Method.

Conform will scale the replacement graphic until it takes on the same dimensions as the placeholder image without concern for the replacement graphic's original width/height proportions. I almost never use this setting since it will distort the image unless it perfectly matches with the width/height proportions of the placeholder image.

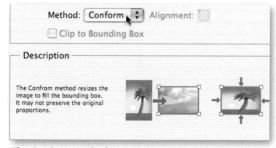

The Conform Method.

Once you've determined the scaling method, you should indicate whether the replacement graphics should be centered or aligned to one of the edges of the placeholder image. You can do that by clicking on the corresponding square in the alignment grid that is displayed to the right of the **Method** pop-up menu. (The Conform scaling method does not offer an alignment setting.)

Assigning Multiple Variable Types to a Layer

You're not limited to defining a single Variable type to each layer. For instance, you might want to assign a Text Replacement Variable to the e-mail address text on a business card template and also assign a Visibility Variable so you can easily hide the text for people who do not have e-mail addresses. The only time you won't be able to assign two types of Variables is when the layer to which you're assigning a Variable does not contain text or a graphic (an Adjustment Layer, for example). In those cases, you'll only be able to assign a Visibility Variable.

Naming Variables

If you're anything like most Photoshop users I encounter, then your layers most likely have creative names like 'Layer 1' because you're either too efficient or too lazy to spend the time to think about layer names. You definitely don't want to continue with this practice when naming Variables, because later you're going to have to type the names into other programs. Here are a few tips to use when naming a Variable:

Use a descriptive name so it's easy to figure out what the Variable refers to (for instance, "logo visibility" is much better than the default "VisibilityVariable1"). This becomes essential when you start creating the Data Sets that are used to define the replacement text and graphics.

> **NOTE**
>
> **Which Are Variables?**
> *You can easily tell which layers have been defined as Variables and which ones haven't by clicking on the Layer pop-up menu at the top of the Define Variables dialog box. Layer names with an asterisk (*) next to them have Variables attached, while those with no asterisk, have no Variables attached.*

Stick with lower case since the Variable names are case sensitive and the names between the Variable and the Data Set must match perfectly, otherwise you'll receive an error message. Sticking with all lower case letters will ensure that you never receive an error message due to a capitization mismatch between files.

Use short names because you'll need to remember the names when switching back and forth between Photoshop and the program you use to define the Data Sets that determine the text and graphics that will replace your placeholders.

Replace spaces with underscores because Variable names cannot contain spaces (for instance "e-mail address" becomes "e-mail_address").

Watch the first letter because Variable names cannot start with a number, a period or a hyphen.

Don't use special characters because Variable names are limited to letters, numbers and only the following special characters: periods (.), hyphens (-), underscores (_) and colons (:).

All this might sound a bit complicated, but if you simply stick to using letters and numbers and use underscores whenever you'd usually use a space, then you should be fine.

Special Considerations

Below are two situations when you'll need to think outside the box when defining Variables:

File Name Variable

In the end, the purpose of using Variables is to have Photoshop quickly create numerous graphic files. At some point Photoshop will have to figure out what names to use for all those graphic files. If you don't think ahead, you'll end up with names like "business card 1." To avoid overly generic names, I suggest you create an extra text layer and hide it in the Layers stack by turning off the eyeball icon for that layer. You can then define a Text Replacement Variable for that layer that will be used to define the file name of the graphic files Photoshop will generate. That way you'll be able to get custom names for each graphic file and end

up with more useful names like "Ben Willmore's Business Card." I'll show you how to define the file names near the end of this chapter.

Linked Variables

If you want to use an element (text or graphic) in multiple areas of the template (let's say a logo is used in two places of the template), then you'll want to link the Variable assigned to one layer to other layers that should contain the same content. You can do that by clicking on the pop-up menu that appears to the right of the Variable name field and choosing the name of a Variable that is already being used by a different layer. Once you've done that, a link symbol will appear to the right of the Variable name indicating that the layer is using the same Variable as another layer.

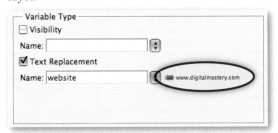

The link symbol indicates that two layers have the same Variable assigned and will therefore be replaced with the same text or graphic.

Now that you know how to properly define Variables, let's take a look at how you define the text and graphics that will be used to replace the placeholders you have in your template file.

Create Data Sets

Once you have a template file created and have defined as many Variables as you see fit, it's time to define the text and graphics that will be used to replace your placeholder layers. All Photoshop needs is a simple text file, but creating the beast isn't as easy as you might expect. Rather than talking you through it while you attempt to construct a file in your head, I think it will be easier to understand what's needed by looking at a simple sample.

name	displaylogo	mugshot
Ben Willmore	TRUE	ben.jpg
Regina Cleveland	TRUE	regina.jpg
Nik Willmore	FALSE	nik.jpg
Nate Willmore	FALSE	nate.tif

This spreadsheet file contains data that will be used to control a Text Replacement Variable, a Visibility Variable and a Pixel Replacement Variable.

```
name,displaylogo,mugshot
Ben Willmore,TRUE,ben.jpg
Regina Cleveland,TRUE,regina.jpg
Nik Willmore,FALSE,nik.jpg
Nate Willmore,FALSE,nate.tif
```

The same sample file viewed as a tab-delimited text file looks a lot more complicated even though it contains the exact same data.

Take a look at the example shown above. The first line is a simple list of the three Variables that were defined in a template file (matching the exact spelling and capitalization perfectly). Each of the lines below the top one is known as a Data Set. This text file is first imported into the template file, and then exported, creating separate graphic files for each Data Set.

Three types of Variables are getting their data from this file. The left-most column is a Text Replacement Variable called 'name,' the middle column is for a Visibility Variable called 'displaylogo' (an entry of TRUE causes the layer to be visible, while FALSE causes the same layer to become hidden), and the right-most column is for a Pixel Replacement Variable called 'mugshot' (where the text matches the file names for images that are stored in the same folder as the text file).

The order of the columns is unimportant as long as the Variable names match the position of the data that is appropriate for each Variable. That's nice for those times when you can obtain a text file that contains that data you need (like an employee directory) because all you have to do is tailor the first line so that it corresponds to the proper data in the file.

So far the concept might seem simple (because it is), but there are some things that can make the creation of a proper text file more difficult. First off, Photoshop needs a text file where entries are separated by either commas or tab characters (the commas and tabs are known as 'delimiters,' and the text files we will be working with are referred to as comma-delimited or tab-delimited files). The example above has everything organized into nice columns and was prepared in a word processor using tabs to delineate between the columns. It was then saved as a text file, as opposed to the word processor's native file format. Let's see what the same data looks like when it's saved as a comma-delimited text file. If you compare the two examples, you'll see that it's essentially the same data.

Now let's look at some special situations you might run into when creating a text file:

Watch for commas that are part of addresses or other text entries. "7157 Magnolia Drive, Nederland CO, 80466" is a properly formatted street address, but since Photoshop thinks of commas as things that separate one entry from the next, it will read the text as "7157 Magnolia Drive" in one entry, "Nederland CO" in a second entry, and "80466" in a third entry. To prevent this problem, enclose the entire address in quotes. When quotes are used, Photoshop ignores any commas, tabs or carriage returns that appear between the quotation characters.

Watch for line breaks. A return character indicates a new Data Set, so if you have a multi-line address like the one below, it will break into multiple entries. So, again, be sure to enclose the entire address in quotes.
"1060 West Addison St.
Chicago, IL 60612"

Watch for quotes because as you've just learned, Photoshop will treat them as an instruction to ignore commas and tabs and will not display them as part of a text replacement layer. So, if your friend is known as Ben "Pixelhead" Willmore, the entry will come into Photoshop as Ben Pixelhead Willmore with no quotes. The solution is to use double quotes by surrounding the entire entry with another set of quotation marks like this "Ben "Pixelhead" Willmore". That will cause Photoshop to leave the text between the outer quotation marks unchanged.

Spaces are ignored if they appear immediately before or after a comma or tab character that separates entries. If you really need a space at the beginning or end of an entry (where the commas would appear), then enclose the entire entry in quotes.

Watch for empty entries where two commas appear with nothing in between them. Every Variable must have a value, so you can't use ",," to indicate that you don't want to replace a string of text or a graphic file.

Watch for capitalization differences between the Variable name as it was defined in Photoshop and how it is used in the text file. The two must match perfectly. A single capitalization difference is enough to prevent the entire process from working. For that reason, I once again suggest you stick with lowercase and use short and simple descriptive names.

Empty equals an error because all entries must contain data, so if you'd like to leave a Text Replacement Variable empty, be sure to place a space between two quotation marks (" ") so Photoshop doesn't ignore the space altogether. You can use the same trick for a Pixel Replacement Variable when you want to prevent a graphic from being replaced.

Location is everything when it comes to graphics files. Using a name like "ben.jpg" will cause Photoshop to assume that the referenced graphics file is in the same folder as the text file that's being fed to Photoshop. If the graphic file is located elsewhere, you'll have to include the path needed to find the file (for example: Hard Drive/Users: Ben/Documents/ben.jpg).

The first Variable is important because it is the only Variable that will be used to give each Data Set a name. That name will be part of the final file name (more on this later). I like to use a hidden layer for this first field so I'm free to put any content into it without fear of that content appearing in the final graphic files that are generated.

For the clean, trouble-free text files, I suggest that you create your Data Sets text file using a spreadsheet program (like Excel). Spreadsheet programs don't try to add spaces after commas and check for punctuation errors like many word processors do (which can wreak havoc on a cleanly formatted text file). Just make sure that when you're done you save the file as a tab or comma-delimited text file .

Okay, we've gone through the steps needed to create a proper text file, so now let's see what's involved with loading it into Photoshop and previewing the results you get when the data replaces the placeholder text and graphics in your template file.

Preview Results

To preview the results of applying a text file to a template image, choose **Image>Variables>Data Sets**. This allows you to load a text file, examine and edit its contents, preview the resulting graphic files and add additional Data Sets, all from a single dialog box.

To load a text file of Data Sets, click the *Import* button that appears on the right side of the dialog box. That will cause the Import Data Set dialog box to appear. That's where you can specify the location of the file you'd like to load, indicate if the first Variable should be used to name the individual Data Sets (as I mentioned earlier, this feature is useful when you want to control the final file name, amongst other things) and decide if you'd like to replace the Data Sets that were previously loaded (you should be able to get away with leaving the encoding pop-up menu to **Automatic**).

The Import Data Set dialog box can be accessed by choosing Image>Variables>Data Sets and then clicking on the Import button in the resulting dialog box.

When you click the OK button, Photoshop will attempt to match up the data in the text file with the Variables that have been defined in your template file. If all is successful, you'll get a preview of the first graphic file that is based on the first Data Set in the text file, and you'll be able to cycle through the Data Sets (using the right and left arrow buttons near the top of the dialog box).

Possible Errors

Alas, success is not guaranteed, so let's look at the error messages you might encounter and how to get around them:

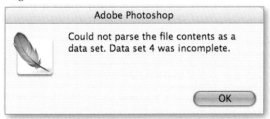

This message will appear when your text file does not contain enough data for all the Variables defined.

Incomplete Data

This error message will appear if your text file does not contain enough entries to feed all the Variables that are defined in the template file. There are two main culprits that usually cause this message to appear: Either you didn't list all the Variables in the first line of the text file, or one of the entries in one of the Data Sets is empty (two commas with nothing in between them). Fortunately, the message will usually indicate which Data Set is deficient so you don't have to check the entire file. In the example message shown on this page, it's Data Set #4, which means the fifth line of the text file needs to be checked (remember, the first line is just a list of Variable names and the second line contains the first real data).

Too Much Data

This error message will appear when there are either more Variable names listed in the first line of the text file than there are Variables defined in the template file, or when one or more of the Data Sets contains too many commas. This is

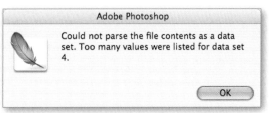

This message will appear when your text file either contains too many Variable names, or too many commas.

very common when addresses contain commas and they have not been placed between quotation marks (see the section on creating Data Sets for more information). As with the previous error message, this one will usually let you know which Data Set is the culprit.

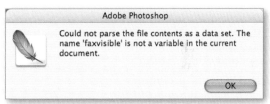

This message will appear when the Variable names listed in the first line of a text file do not perfectly match the Variables defined in the template file.

Variable Name Mismatch

This error message will appear when a Variable name found in the first line of the text file either doesn't perfectly match the name of a Variable in the template file (keep on eye on capitalization in that case), or is nonexistent in the template file.

The Data Sets portion of the Variables dialog box after a successful import of data from a text file.

Check for Data and Layout Problems

Once you've successfully imported a text file, you should see how it is interacting with the placeholder layers of the template file. You can do that by cycling through the different Data Sets (using the right and left arrow buttons to the right of the **Data Set** pop-up menu). While you view the different Data Sets, keep on eye on your template file to see if any text is being truncated, or if there are any typos in the data that's being applied (make sure the *Preview* checkbox is turned on, otherwise you won't see any results). If you encounter any problems, you can modify the Data Sets by choosing the Variable you'd like to work with and modifying the Value field that appears just below the Variable's name. You can also click the *Apply* button to embed the Data Sets into the template file and then click OK to return to your template (just clicking OK without clicking *Apply* would trash the Data Sets and force you to re-import them before being able to preview the file again). Then you can adjust the layout to accommodate problems like lengthy text that you didn't anticipate when creating the template.

Once you are confident that everything is working correctly, you can stop previewing and actually create individual graphic files for each Data Set.

Manual Data Sets

You can add Data Sets to a template file within Photoshop (they don't have to come from an external text file). To add a Data Set to the active template file, choose **Image>Variables>Data Sets***, click on the New Data Set icon (it looks like a floppy disc and is located to the left of the trash can icon. This is a very inefficient method for entering a lot of data, so I mainly use it when I notice that an external text file does not contain a Data Set that I need.*

Generate Graphics

If you were able to successfully preview the Data Set within the template file, you should be ready to have Photoshop create individual graphics files for each Data Set found in the text file.

Exporting Data Sets

To start the process, choose **File>Export>Data Sets As Files**. If you find that the menu is grayed out, then it means that there are no Data Sets currently loaded (you most likely clicked OK without clicking the *Apply* button in the last dialog box). If that's the case, then choose **File>Import>Variable Data Sets** and feed it your text file just as you did in the Data Sets area of the Variables dialog box (the thing you did earlier where you could have clicked *Apply* to attach the Data Set to your template file).

Save Options

The top portion of the dialog box allows you to specify where you would like the resulting graphic files to be saved. You also have the choice of creating files for all the Data Sets that were contained in the text file, or only exporting a single Data Set as a graphic file (I always leave the Data Sets pop-up menu set to **All Data Sets** because I could have applied a single Data Set using the **Image>Apply Data Set** command).

File Naming

This section allows you to specify a file naming convention for the group of images that will be saved. I usually enter a descriptive name in the first field (like "Business Card"), choose either

The Export dialog box allows you to specify the file names you wish to be used for creating multiple graphic files.

Space or Underscore for the second field and then set the third file to Data Set Name (which will insert the name of each individual Data Set into the end of the file name).

Once you click the OK button, Photoshop will start processing the data from the text file you imported and will create a separate graphic file for each of the Data Sets that were contained in the text file. Each of these files will be a layered Photoshop file format image that will be saved to the location you specified at the top of the dialog box.

You can apply the same text file to multiple template files (business card, letterhead and envelope, for example). Just make sure all the templates contain all the Variables that are defined in the Data Set (simply hide layers that shouldn't be part of the final image).

NOTE

Flattened Files
If you need flattened versions of the graphics files, consider making an action that simply flattens the image and then apply it through the new Image Processor feature that is covered in Chapter 10 (which allows you to quickly apply the action and then automatically save the file in TIFF or JPEG file format.)

Consider ImageReady
You can also process your template file from ImageReady (which comes bundled with Photoshop). This will allow you to save the images in any of the following file formats:
JPG   GIF
PNG   SWF

I'd like to say that if you feel a little befuddled after trying to digest all of this in one sitting, I wouldn't worry too much. Once you've given this thing a thorough test drive, you'll see for yourself how all the elements interact with each other, and it should be a lot less confusing. The time you spend learning this feature is priceless, because when you've got a project that is a good candidate for Variables, this incredibly powerful tool can save you hours if not days of your life.

Index

Numbers

1-column Toolbar, 49, 54, 56
2-column Toolbar, 49, 54, 56
2-monitor setup, 7, 16
3rd-party filters, 102
16-bit images, 100
32-bit images, 76–77, 100
32-bit layers, 77

A

Accent Color pop-up menu, 6
Acrobat Connect meetings, 7–9
Add Noise filter, 77
Add to Favorites checkbox, 25
Add to Selection mode, 84-86
Add to Swatches button, 124
Adjust tab, 27, 38
adjustments, Lightroom, 42
adjustment icon, 31
Adjustment Layers
  Black & White, 74, 75
  Brightness/Contrast, 79
  Curves, 72
  and presets, 72
  and retouching tools, 88
  and Shadow/Highlight
  adjustments, 80
  and Smart Filters, 80, 100
  and Variation adjustments, 80
adjustment tools, 59–80
  Black & White, 59, 73–75
  Black/White Point, 69–70
  brightness/contrast,
  38, 60, 62–65, 78–79
  Channel Mixer, 79–80
  color picker, 76
  Curves, 59, 61–72
  Levels, 61, 69, 79
  Merge to HDR, 76, 77
  Shadow/Highlights, 80

Smart Filters, 80, 97–102
Variations, 80
Adjustments menu, 59, 100, 102
Adobe Acrobat Connect, 7, 8–9
Adobe Device Central,
  25, 116–117
Adobe DNG Converter, 20
Adobe Fireworks, 115
Adobe Flash, 117, 128
Adobe Illustrator, 116
Adobe ImageReady, 115
Adobe Photo Downloader.
  See Photo Downloader
Adobe Photographers Directory,
  7–8
Adobe Photoshop.
  See Photoshop
Adobe Photoshop Lightroom,
  27, 42, 47
Adobe Stock Photos feature, 24
Advanced section, Preferences
  dialog box, 4, 5
alignment
  image, 76
  layer, 105–106
All Layers setting, Sample menu,
  89
Allow Multi-surface Operations
  option, 120
Angle setting
  Clone Source palette, 94
  Vanishing Point dialog box,
  118, 119
aperture setting, 17
Apply Camera Raw Settings
  command, 4
Apply Image command, 77
Apply Presets submenu, 46
arrows, double, 51
aspect ratios, 11
Auto-Align Layers command, 97,
  105–106, 107, 112

Auto-Alignment feature, 76
Auto-Blend Layers command, 97,
  107, 112
Auto button
  Black & White dialog box, 75
  Camera Raw, 28, 44
Auto checkboxes, 28
Auto-Collapse Icon Palettes
  option, 53, 122
Auto-Enhance feature, 85–86
Auto Hide checkbox, 91
Auto Levels command, 75
Auto option, Auto-Align Layers,
  105
Automate menu, 76, 112
Average filter, 77

B

Background Eraser tool, 84
Balance slider, Split Toning, 45
Baseline checkbox, 71
Basic icon, 27, 38
Basic tab, 27, 38–40
Batch command, 22
Bit-Depth pop-up menu, 77
Black & White Adjustment
  Layers, 74, 75
Black & White converter,
  59, 73–75, 104
Black Point slider, 69–70
Blacks slider, 27, 37, 38, 39
Blend Images Together, 112
blending modes, 92, 98, 102–
  105
Blending sliders, 101
Blue curve, 66
Blue slider, 79
Blur filters, 77
Box Blur filter, 77
brackets, exposure, 15
Breeze meetings, 8

Bridge, 3–25
  adjusting JPEG/TIFF, 22–23
  aspect ratios available in, 11
  and Camera Raw, 4, 22–23
  comparing images in, 16
  Content panel, 12–15
  downloading photos from camera with, 18
  enabling color mgmt, 14
  Favorites panel, 7–9
  feature changes, 3–5
  Filter panel, 10–11
  Folders panel, 7
  generating thumbnails in, 13
  how thumbnails are displayed by, 12
  Inspector panel, 17, 24
  interface changes, 5–7
  Keywords panel, 17
  magnifying portion of image in, 16–17, 24
  merging images in, 76
  Metadata panel, 17
  Preferences dialog box, 24
  Preview panel, 16–17
  Ratings panel, 14
  rearranging panels in, 6
  Slideshow feature, 23–24
  starting a meeting from, 8–9
Bridge Center, 4
Bridge CS3 menu
  Camera Raw Preferences command, 42, 44
  Prefer Adobe Camera Raw for JPEG and TIFF Files checkbox, 31
  Preferences command, 3, 5, 13, 14
Bridge Home, 4
Brighter Color blending mode, 105
brightness adjustment, 38, 62–63, 78–79
Brightness/Contrast dialog box, 60, 78–79
brightness range, analyzing, 67–68
Brightness slider, 37, 78
brush sizes, 85

C

cache, 4, 5, 13, 123
Calculations command, 77
Calibrate tab, 27
camera
  cleaning sensor on, 37
  downloading photos from, 18
  red-eye reduction feature, 31
  resolution, 95
  serial number, 11
  settings, 17
Camera Calibration icon, 27
Camera Calibration tab, 30
Camera Raw, 27–47
  adjusting curves in, 41
  adjusting JPEG/TIFF files in, 22–23, 29–31
  adjusting/removing color in, 43–44
  and Bridge, 4, 22–23
  clipping display, 29
  Full Screen mode, 28
  icons, 27
  and Photoshop Lightroom, 42
  Preferences dialog box, 28
  and Quick Thumbnails, 12
  Red Eye tool, 31–32
  Retouch tool, 33–38
  retouching multiple images in, 36–37
  saving settings in, 46
  sliders, 28, 38–40
  and Smart Objects, 46–47
  tabs, 27
  Update DNG Previews, 47
  workflow settings, 28
Camera Raw dialog box
  Full Screen icon, 28
  Highlight checkbox, 29
  HSL/Grayscale tab, 43–44
  illustrated, 30
  Preview checkbox, 46
  Shadow checkbox, 28, 29
  Split Toning tab, 45
  Tone Curve tab, 41
  triangle icon, 28, 29
camera serial number, filtering images by, 11
camera settings, 17
Canvas Size command, 77

card reader, downloading, 18
cell phones, 25, 115, 116
Centralized Cache File, 5
Channel Mixer, 73, 79–80
channel overlays, 71
Channels pop-up menu, 65–66, 68, 71
Check for Device Updates, 116
Choose Custom Color, 55
Clip Operations to Surface Edges option, 120
clipping, 29, 74
clipping display
  Camera Raw, 29
  Curves, 70
  Levels, 69
clipping mask, 100
Clone setting, 34–35
clone source icons, 90
Clone Source palette, 90–94
  Angle setting, 94
  Auto Hide checkbox, 91
  illustrated, 90
  keyboard shortcuts, 93
  Offset setting, 93
  Opacity setting, 91
  Overlay Mode menu, 91
  purpose of, 83
  Rotate setting, 93
  Scale setting, 93
  Show Overlay settings, 91
  storing clone sources in, 90
  using with retouching tools, 35
  Width/Height settings, 94
Clone Stamp tool, 35, 83, 89, 90
Close Stack command, 15
Clouds filter, 77
CMYK mode, 62, 65, 75
Collapse All Stacks command, 15
Collections, 4, 25
color casts, 102
color channels, 65–66, 71
color correction, 29
color curves, 65
Color Handling pop-up menu, 121
color intensity, 76
color management
  enabling in Bridge, 14
  and Print dialog box, 121
  and Quick Thumbnails, 12

Color Mode pop-up menu, 77
color modes, 65, 77
color picker, 55, 74, 76
Color Picker dialog box, 76, 124
color printers, 121
Color Range tool, 84
color separations, 75
color shifts, 65–66, 71
color sliders, 73–74
color tints, 74
colors
adding to Swatches palette, 124
adjusting, 43–44
Bridge, 5–6
changing surround, 54–55
darkening, 102–103
lightening, 102–103
previewing, 121
remapping, 105
removing, 40, 44, 73–75, 104
replacing, 103
comparing images, 16
composite curves, 65
Compression checkbox, 21
connected planes, 118
Content panel, 12–15, 16
Content tab, 12
Content Type pop-up menu, 116
Contract command, 87
contrast adjustment, 63–64, 68, 75, 78–79
Contrast setting, Refine Edge, 86
Contrast slider, 37, 39, 78
Convert for Smart Filters command, 98
Convert to DNG checkbox, 19
Convert to Grayscale, 40, 44
Convert to Linear Image, 21
Convert to Profile command, 124
Convert to Smart Object command, 47, 98, 99, 128
Convert to sRGB option, 124
Copy command, 13
Copy Settings command, 22
"Copy to" submenu, 13
copying & pasting images, 13
copyrights, photo, 11, 22
corner, bending image around, 120

Create Metadata Template command, 22
Create Plane tool, 118, 119
Create Subfolders pop-up menu, 19
Crop command, 77
Current & Below setting, Sample menu, 89, 90
Current Layer setting, Sample menu, 89
Curve Display Options icon, 59, 60, 62, 66
Curve tab, 27
curves
adding points to, 64–65, 68
changing angle of, 63–64
changing height of, 62–63
color, 65
composite, 65
controlling shape of, 41
flattening, 68
loading saved, 60
saving as presets, 60, 72
Curves Adjustment Layer, 72
Curves dialog box, 59–72
adjusting brightness in, 62–63
adjusting contrast in, 63–64, 68
as alternative to Levels, 61, 69
Baseline checkbox, 71
Black/White Point sliders, 69–70
Channel Overlays checkbox, 71
Channels pop-up menu, 65–66, 68, 71
Clipping Display checkbox, 70
expanding, 67
Histogram, 67–68
icons, 59
illustrated, 60
in-depth information on, 61
Intersection Line checkbox, 69
learning to use, 61–66
Load & Save buttons, 60
power/versatility of, 61
Preset pop-up menu, 60, 72
switching between Light and Ink settings in, 62
turning off checkboxes in, 60
Cylindrical option, Auto-Align Layers, 106, 108, 109

D

Darken mode, 102
Darken slider, 32
Darker Color mode, 103, 104
Darks slider, 41
De-Interlace filter, 77
Deactivate command, 116
demosaicing, 21
Desktop, 7
Detail icon, 27
Detail tab, 27, 30
Develop Settings, 4, 22
Device Central button, 116
Device Central, 25, 115–117
Device Central Online, 117
Devices menu, 116
dialog boxes
Black and White, 73
Brightness/Contrast, 60, 78–79
Channel Mixer, 80
Color Picker, 76, 124
Curves. See Curves dialog box
DNG Conversion Settings, 21
File Info, 25
Hue/Saturation, 68
Image Size, 124
Levels, 61, 69, 79
Merge to HDR, 76, 77
New, 77
PDF Presentation, 124–125
Photo Downloader, 18
Preferences, 24, 122–123. See also Preferences dialog box
Print, 121
Print with Preview, 116, 121
Refine Edge, 86
Save for Web & Devices, 116–117
Slideshow Options, 23
Vanishing Point, 118–120
Difference Clouds filter, 77
Digimarc filter, 100
digital camera. See also camera
cleaning sensor on, 37
downloading photos from, 18
resolution, 95
Digital Negatives, 19. See also DNG files

digital noise, 11
Displace filter, 102
Distributed Cache File setting, 5
DNG Conversion Settings dialog
    box, 21
DNG Converter, Adobe, 20
DNG files, 19–21
    compressing, 21
    converting RAW files to, 19–21
    default settings for, 21
    embedded previews, 19, 21
    Photo Downloader settings, 21
    and Photoshop Lightroom, 42
    pros and cons of, 19–20
    updating JPEG preview in, 47
dock icon, 50
docks
    auto-show feature, 53
    collapsing, 52–53
    creating, 52
    defined, 50
    populating, 52
    purpose of, 52
    removing palettes from, 53
    resizing palettes in, 52
    using multiple, 52
double arrows, 51
double triangle icon, 59
drag-selecting thumbnails, 13
Duplicate command, 77
Duplicate Layer command, 47
dust specks, 33, 36, 37
dynamic range, 76

E

Edit menu
    Apply Camera Raw Settings, 4
    Auto-Align Layers, 105–106
    Auto-Blend Layers, 107
    Convert to Profile, 124
    Copy command, 13
    Develop Settings command, 4
    Device Central command, 116
    Fade command, 98
    File Info command, 22
    Fill command, 77
    Find command, 4, 25
    Free Transform command, 77
    Generate High Quality
        Thumbnail command, 13

Generate Quick Thumbnail, 13
Keyboard Shortcuts, 75
Paste command, 13
Preferences, 3, 5, 13, 14
Refine Edge command, 86–88
Show All Files command, 4
Show Camera Raw Files Only
    command, 4
Show Graphic Files Only
    command, 4
Show Metadata Placard, 4
Show Vector Files Only
    command, 4
Stroke command, 77
Transform command, 77
Edit Plane tool, 118
Edit>Find dialog box, 4, 25
editing
    metadata-based, 33
    Smart Filter settings, 98
    Smart Object contents, 100
    video, 90
Edit>Transform menu, 101
Embed Original Raw File setting,
    20, 21
Emboss filter, 77, 102
Emulator mode, Device Central,
    117
Enable Color Management in
    Bridge setting, 14
Enable Large Document Format
    (.psb) checkbox, 123
EnableAllPluginsForSmart Filters.
    jsx, 102
EPS files, 11
Eraser tools, 84, 95
Expand All Stacks command, 15
Expand command, 87
Export Transparent Image
    feature, 115
exposure compensation setting,
    17
exposure settings, 15
Exposure slider, 38
Extended features, 128–129
ExtendScript Toolkit, 128
Extensis Portfolio, 47
Extract command, 84
Extract filter, 100
Eyedropper tool, 95

F

facial retouching, 92
Fade command, 98
Favorites panel, 7–9
Feather command, 83, 87
Feather setting, Refine Edge, 87
feedback icons, 51
file browser, 7. See also Bridge
file creation date, 4
file formats
    for 32-bit images, 77
    and Device Central, 116
File Handling section,
    Preferences dialog box, 123
File Info command, 22, 25
File menu
    File Info command, 25
    Get Info command, 124
    Get Photos from Camera
        command, 18
    New command, 77
    New Document command, 116
    Open in Camera Raw command,
        22, 23, 29
    Print command, 121
    Recent Items list, 24
    Return to Photoshop, 117
    Save As command, 31
    Save for Web & Devices
        command, 116
    Test in Device Central
        command, 116
file type, filtering by, 11
File>Automate menu, 76, 112
File>Export menu, 116, 125
files
    copying, 7, 13
    loading into stack, 126
    locking, 14
    moving, 7, 14
    placing on Desktop, 7
    rejecting, 14
    saving as collections, 4, 25
File>Scripts menu, 107, 126
Fill command, 77
Fill Light slider, 27, 38, 39
film speed, 17, 129.
    See also ISO setting
Filmstrip Focus command, 4

Filter menu, 3, 10, 77, 98
Filter panel, 4, 10–11
filters. *See also Smart Filters*
  32-bit mode, 77
  applying to layers, 97–100
  and bit depth, 100
  clearing, 11
  expanding/narrowing scope, 10
  intermixing with adjustments,
  102
  masking, 99–100
  moving/copying between layers,
  99
  specialized uses for, 11
  third-party, 102
  toggling on/off, 10
Filter>Vanishing Point, 118, 120
Find All Files checkbox, 4
Find command, 4, 25
Find dialog box, 25
Fireworks, 115
Flash, 116, 117, 128
folders
  copying and pasting images
  between, 13
  displaying recently viewed, 24
  moving images between, 14
  searching, 10–11
folders list, 7
Folders panel, 7
Free Transform command, 77
Full Screen icon, 28
Full Screen mode, 28, 54, 55

G

Gamut preferences, 123
Gaussian Blur filter, 77
General section, Preferences
  dialog box, 122
Generate High Quality Thumbnail
  command, 13
Generate Quick Thumbnail
  command, 13
Get Info command, 124
Get Photos from Camera
  command, 18
Google maps, 125
Gradient Map command, 105
graphics application, 118
graphics tablets, 13

grayscale images,
  40, 44, 75, 77
Grayscale Toolbar icon, 122
Green curve, 66
Green slider, 79
Group as Stacks command, 15
grouping
  images, 15
  palettes, 50
  panels, 6

H

HDR images, 76–77
Heal setting, Retouch tool,
  34–35
Healing Brush tool, 35, 83, 90
Height setting, Clone Source
  palette, 94
Help menu
  Deactivate command, 116
  Device Central Online
  command, 117
  Export Transparent Image
  feature, 115
  Resize Image command, 116
  Transfer Activation command,
  116
Help>Welcome Screen menu,
  115
High Dynamic Range, 76
High Pass filter, 77
High Quality Thumbnails,
  12, 23
Highlight checkbox, 28, 29
Highlights slider, 41
Histogram command, 67
histograms, 29, 67–68, 69
History States setting,
  122, 123
HSL/Grayscale tab, 43–44
Hue/Saturation dialog box, 68
Hue slider, 45, 74
Hue tab, HSL/Grayscale, 43

I

Ignore Adjustment Layers icon,
  89, 90
Illustrator, 116
Image Backdrop slider, 5
Image Conversion Method
  setting, 21
image libraries, cataloging, 42
Image menu, 77
image processing application, 27
Image Processor command, 126
Image Size command, 77
Image Size dialog box, 124
Image Stacks feature, 128–129
image thumbnails. *See
  thumbnails*
Image>Adjustments menu, 100,
  102
ImageReady, 115
images. *See also photos*
  32-bit, 76–77
  adjusting brightness/contrast
  of, 38, 62–65, 68, 75, 78–79
  adjusting colors in,
  43–44, 65–66
  aligning, 76
  aspect ratios for, 11
  attaching copyright notice to,
  11, 22
  bending around corner, 120
  changing surround color for,
  54–55
  color correcting, 29
  combining multiple,
  107–112, 129
  comparing, 16
  converting color to black &
  white, 73–75
  copying and pasting between
  folders, 13
  demosaicing, 21
  embedding metadata in, 22
  grouping into stacks, 15
  High Dynamic Range (HDR),
  76–77
  including photo credits with, 11
  loading into stack, 126, 128
  locking, 14
  magnifying portion of, 16–17,
  24

merging, 77
moving between folders, 14
panoramic. *See panoramas*
previewing multiple, 16
rejecting, 14
removing color from, 40, 44,
73–75, 104
removing defects from, 33–38
resizing, 116
searching for, 10–11, 25
selecting series of, 13
showing metadata with,
124–125
showing on two-monitor setup,
7
viewing labeled/unlabeled, 4
zooming in on, 17, 24
**Include Non-Indexed Files option,
25**
Info command, 66, 74
Info palette, 66, 74
Ink setting, Curves, 62
Inspector panel, 17, 24
intensity, color, 76
**Interactive Layout option, 109,
112**
interface colors, Bridge, 5–6
**Interface section, Preferences
dialog box, 122**
Interpolation menu, 124
Intersection Line checkbox, 69
Inverse command, 77
Invert command, 104
ISO setting, 11, 17, 129
ISO Speed Ratings, 11
iView, Microsoft, 47

J

jaggy edges, 85, 121
JPEG files
adjusting in Camera Raw,
22–23, 29–31
embedding metadata in, 31
JPEG Preview options, 21

K

Keyboard Language setting, 24
keyboard shortcuts
for accessing Black & White
dialog box, 75
for clearing filters, 11
for Clone Source palette
settings, 93
for copying images, 13
for deleting rejected images, 14
for displaying overlays, 91
for grouping images into stacks,
15
for grouping panels, 6
for locking files, 14
for magnifying images, 16
for moving images, 14
for producing Adjustment
Layers, 75
for resetting color sliders, 74
for screen modes, 54, 55
for selection modes, 84
for showing/hiding palettes, 51
for toggling Preview checkbox,
73
**Keyboard Shortcuts command,
75**
Keywords panel, 4, 17
Kodak PhotoCD format, 124

L

Lab mode, 75
Label menu, 3, 14
landscapes, 75
Large Document Format files, 77
Lasso tool, 83
Layer Effects icon, 97, 101
layer masks, 101
Layer>Adjustment Layers menu
Black & White command, 104
Gradient Map command, 105
Invert command, 104
Layer>Layer Style menu, 101
**Layer>New Adjustment Layer
menu, 100**
Layer>Rasterize menu, 100
layers, 97–112. *See also*
Adjustment Layers
applying filters to, 97–100

auto-aligning, 105–106, 107
ignoring, 90
moving/copying filters, 99
rasterizing, 100
sampling from, 88
Layers palette, 51, 90, 92
Layer>Smart Objects menu
Convert to Smart Object
command, 98, 99, 128
New Smart Object via Copy
command, 47
Lens Blur filter, 102
Lens Corrections icon, 27
Lens Corrections tab, 30
Lens Flare filter, 77
Lens tab, 27
Levels dialog box, 61, 69, 79
Light setting, Curves, 62
Light Table command, 4
Lightbox command, 4
Lighten mode, 102
Lighter Color mode, 103–105
Lighting Effects filter, 102
**Lightroom, Photoshop, 27, 42,
47**
Lights slider, 41
linear DNG files, 21
Liquify filter, 100
Load button, Curves, 60
**Load Files Into Stack command,
107, 112, 126**
Load Preset command, 60, 72
Load Selection command, 77
lock icon, 14
loupe views, 16–17
**Luminance tab, HSL/Grayscale,
43**

M

Macromedia, 8
Magic Eraser tool, 95
Magic Wand tool, 83, 84, 95
magnifying images, 16–17, 24
maps, Google, 125
marching ants, 87
Mask Mode icon, 88
mask overlays, 100
masking filters, 99–100
masks, layer, 101
Match Print Colors, 121

Maximized Screen Mode, 54, 55
Maximum filter, 77
Median mode, 128, 129
meetings, on-line, 8–9
Memory Usage setting, 123
Merge to HDR dialog box, 76–77
merging images, 76, 77
metadata
    defined, 31
    embedding in images, 22, 31
    recording retouching in, 38
    showing in PDF presentations,
      124–125
    templates, 22
metadata-based edits, 33
Metadata panel, 4, 17
Metadata placard, 17
metering mode icons, 17
Microsoft iView, 47
Microsoft Office, 8
Minimum filter, 77
mobile devices, 115, 116.
    See also cell phones
Mode pop-up menu, 91
Modify Border command, 77
Modify menu, 83, 87
monitor resolution, 56
Monochrome checkbox, 79
Motion Blur filter, 77
"Move to" submenu, 14
Multi-surface Operations, 120
multiple images
    combining, 107–112, 129
    previewing, 16
    retouching, 36–37
multiple shooters, 11

N

New dialog box, 77
New Document command, 116
New Preset icon, 46
New Selection mode, 84
New Smart Object via Copy, 47
New Synchronized Window, 6
No Folder icon, 4
No Label option, 4
"No" symbol, 11
noise reduction, 11, 129
Non-Indexed Files option, 25
NTSC Colors filter, 77

O

Office, Microsoft, 8
Offset filter, 77
Offset setting, Clone Source
    palette, 93
On Black Mode icon, 88
on-line meetings, 8–9
On White Mode icon, 88
one-column Toolbar, 49, 54, 56
Opacity setting, 87, 91
Open in Camera Raw command,
    22, 29
Open in Photoshop as Smart
    Objects checkbox, 46
Open Stack command, 15
Open with Rosetta checkbox,
    124
OpenEXR format, 77
Options bar
    Auto-Enhance checkbox, 85
    Ignore Adjustment Layers icon,
      89
    illustrated, 56
    Sample All Layers checkbox,
      84, 88, 89
    Sample pop-up menu, 89
    Sample Size setting, 95
    Workspace menu, 56
Overlay Mode menu, 91
overlays
    channel, 71
    clone source, 91

P

Paintbucket tool, 54, 95
Palette Docks, 52–53. See also
    docks
palette menus, 50
Palette Well, 49, 50, 53
palettes, 49–53
    accessing, 50
    accessing side menus for, 50
    auto-collapsing, 53
    closing, 51
    collapsing into icons, 50, 52
    cycling between fields in, 51
    defined, 50
    vs. groups, 50

minimizing, 50, 51
removing from dock, 53
repositioning, 51
resizing, 51, 52
saving as Workspace, 56
showing/hiding, 51, 53
snapping, 50
stacking, 49
storing in dock, 52
terminology, 50
working with collapsed, 53
panels, 6. See also specific
    panels
panoramas, 11, 15, 105–106,
    107–111
Parametric curves, 41
Paste command, 13, 120
Paste Settings command, 22
Patch tool, 35
Pattern Maker filter, 100
PDF Presentation dialog box,
    124–125
Performance section,
    Preferences dialog box, 123
Perspective option, Auto-Align
    Layers, 105, 108, 109
photo credits, 11
Photo Downloader, 18–22
    Advanced Dialog button, 22
    advanced version, 18
    backing up images in, 19
    Create Subfolders pop-up
      menu, 19
    DNG conversion settings, 19,
      21
    embedding metadata in photos
      with, 22
    illustrated, 18
    Import settings, 19
    launching automatically, 18
    Location setting, 19
    Open Adobe Bridge checkbox,
      19
    renaming files in, 19
    "Save Copies to" checkbox,
      19
    sorting photos in, 19
    Source setting, 18
PhotoCD format, 124
photographers
    including photo credits for, 11

searching for, 7–8
Photomerge command, 112
photos. *See also images*
attaching copyright notice to, 11, 22
embedding metadata in, 22, 31
Photoshop
Extended version, 128–129
file format, 77
launch speed, 124
other books about, 43, 61, 65, 76, 98
as Universal Binary application, 124
and Windows Vista, 124
Photoshop command, 76
Photoshop CS2: Up to Speed, 76, 98
Photoshop CS3 Studio Techniques, 43, 61, 65
Photoshop Lightroom, 27, 42, 47
Photoshop Manages Colors option, 121
Pixel Aspect Ratio command, 77
Pixel Doubling feature, 123
pixelation, 121
planes, connected, 118
plug-ins, 102, 124
Point curve, 41, 43
Point Sample setting, 95
Portable Bit Map format, 77
portable devices, testing documents for use on, 25
Portfolio, Extensis, 47
portraits, 75
Prefer Adobe Camera Raw for JPEG and TIFF Files checkbox, 22, 23, 29
Prefer Adobe Camera Raw for JPEG Files checkbox, 123
Prefer Adobe Camera Raw for Supported Raw Files checkbox, 123
Preferences command
Bridge CS3 menu, 3, 5, 13, 14
Edit menu, 3, 5, 13, 14
Preferences dialog box
Advanced section, 4, 5
for Camera Raw, 28

CS2 *vs.* CS3, 122–123
File Handling section, 123
General section, 122
Interface section, 122
Performance section, 123
Startup Scripts section, 5, 24
Thumbnails section, 4, 5
Transparency & Gamut section, 123
Preset pop-up menu
Black & White dialog box, 75
Convert to sRGB option, 124
Curves dialog box, 60, 72
presets
Black & White converter, 75
Camera Raw, 46
Channel Mixer, 79–80
Curves, 60, 72
Presets pop-up menu, 28
Presets tab, 28
Preview checkbox
Black & White converter, 73
Camera Raw dialog box, 46
Preview modes, Refine Edge, 87–88
Preview panel, 16–17
Print dialog box, 121
Print Resolution readout, 121
Print with Preview dialog box, 116, 121
Printer pop-up menu, 121
printers, color, 121
professional photographers, searching for, 7–8
Professional Photographers of America, 7
Promote to Top of Stack command, 15
.psb files, 123
Pupil Size slider, 32
Purge Cache for This Folder command, 5, 13
Purge Central Cache command, 4

Quick Mask icons, 83
Quick Mask Mode icon, 87–88
Quick Selection tool, 83, 84–86
Quick Thumbnails, 12, 13, 23

R

Radial Blur filter, 77, 99
Radiance file format, 77
Radius setting
Refine Edge, 86
Retouch tool, 33
rasterizing layers, 100
Ratings panel, 14
RAW files. *See also Camera Raw*
backing up, 20
Camera Raw processing of, 13
converting to DNG format, 19–23
in-camera processing of, 13
and Preferences dialog box, 123
and Quick Thumbnails, 12
Recent Items list, 24
Recovery slider, 38
Red curve, 65–66
red eye, preventing, 31
Red Eye tool, Camera Raw, 31–32
Red slider, Channel Mixer, 79
Reds slider, Black & White converter, 73–74
Refine Edge button, 86
Refine Edge command, 86–88
Refine Edge dialog box, 86
Refine Edge palette, 83
Refine Selection command, 83
reflections, 70
Refresh command, 4
rejecting files, 14
Remember Palette Locations checkbox, 122
Rename Files pop-up menu, 19
Render Grid option, 116
Repeat Slideshow option, 23
Reposition Only option, Auto-Align Layers, 106, 108, 109
Resize Image command, 116
resolution
digital camera, 95
monitor, 56
print, 121
response curves, 77
Retouch tool, Camera Raw, 33–38

retouching
  with blending modes, 92
  with Camera Raw, 33–38
  with Clone Source palette, 90–94
  on empty layers, 88
  facial, 92
  multiple images, 36–37
retouching tools, 33–38, 83, 88–90
Return to Photoshop command, 117
Reveal Scripts in Finder button, 5
RGB mode, 65, 75
RGB values, 75, 79
Rotate Canvas command, 77
Rotate setting, Clone Source palette, 93

S

Sample All Layers checkbox, 84, 88, 89, 90
Sample pop-up menu, 89–90
Sample Size setting, 95
saturation clipping, 70
Saturation slider, 37, 40, 68, 74
Saturation tab, HSL/Grayscale, 43
Save as Collection option, 4, 25
Save As command, 31
Save button, Curves, 60
Save for Web & Devices command, 116, 124
Save for Web & Devices dialog box, 116–117
Save Image button, 31, 38
Save Palette Locations checkbox, 122
Save Preset command, 60, 72
Save Response Curve button, 77
Save Selection command, 77
Save Workspace command, 56
saved searches, 4
Scale setting, Clone Source palette, 93
scratch disks, 123
screen modes, 54–55
screen redraw, speeding up, 123

scripts
  creating, 128
  for loading files into stack, 126
  startup, 5, 24
Scripts/JavaScript folder, 102
Select Labeled command, 4
Select menu
  Feather command, 83
  Inverse command, 77
  Load Selection command, 77
  Modify Border command, 77
  Refine Edge command, 86–88
  Save Selection command, 77
  Transform Selection command, 77
Select Unlabeled command, 4
selection modes, 84
selections
  adding to, 84, 85
  with Quick Selection tool, 84–86
  subtracting from, 84, 85
Select>Modify menu, 87
separations, color, 75
serial number, filtering by camera, 11
Settings pop-up menu, 28
Shadow checkbox, 28, 29
Shadow/Highlights adjustments, 80
Shadows slider, 27, 38, 41
Shape Blur filter, 77
Shift-Tab, 51
shortcuts. *See keyboard shortcuts*
Show All Files command, 4
Show Camera Raw Files Only command, 4
Show Edges checkbox, 118
Show Graphic Files Only command, 4
Show Menu Colors checkbox, 122
Show Metadata Placard setting, 4, 17
Show Overlay checkbox, 37
Show Overlay settings, 91
Show Reject Files command, 14
Show Tool Tips checkbox, 122
Show Vector Files Only

  command, 4
shutter speed setting, 17
single-column Toolbar, 49, 54, 56
Slide Duration menu, 24
slide shows, 23–24
Slideshow Options dialog box, 23
Smart Filters, 97–102
  and Adjustment Layers, 80, 100
  applying, 98–100
  applying adjustments via, 100
  and bit depth, 100
  Blending Slider settings, 101
  changing order of, 99
  changing settings for, 98
  forcing update to, 102
  hiding/showing, 99
  intermixing with adjustments, 102
  masking, 99–100
  moving/copying between layers, 99
  purpose of, 80, 97–98
  setting blending options for, 98
  and third-party filters, 102
  version considerations, 100
  ways of using, 100–102
Smart Object command, 100
Smart Objects
  and Camera Raw, 46–47
  editing contents of, 100
  embedding, 47
  enabling third-party filters for, 102
  extracting layers from, 101
  in-depth coverage of, 98
  nesting, 99
Smart Sharpen filter, 77
Smooth setting, Refine Edge, 86
snapping, 50
Software Rendering setting, 24
Sort pop-up menu, 11
splash screen, 115
Split Toning tab, 45
Spot Removal command, 36
Stack Mode menu, 128
stacking
  images, 15, 126, 128–129

palettes, 49
panels, 6
Stacks menu, 15
Standard mode, Refine Edge, 87
Standard Screen Mode, 54
Start Meeting feature, 8–9
Startup Scripts section,
    Preferences dialog box, 5, 24
Stock Photos, Adobe, 24
Stroke command, 77
sub-folders, searching, 11
Subtract from Selection mode,
    84, 85
Surface Blur filter, 77
Swatches palette, 124

T

Tab key, 51
Temperature slider, 28
Test in Device Central
    command, 116
third-party filters, 102
thumbnails
    changing sort order of, 11
    drag-selecting, 13
    generating, 13
    how Bridge displays, 12
    Quick *vs.* High Quality, 12, 13
    setting preferences for, 4, 5
Thumbnails section, Preferences
    dialog box, 4, 5
thumbtack icon, 11
TIFF files
    adjusting in Camera Raw,
    22–23, 29–31
    embedding metadata in, 31
    saving 32-bit images as, 77
Tint checkbox, 74
Tone Curve icon, 27
Tone Curve tab, 41
Toolbar
    illustrated, 54, 56
    one- *vs.* two-column, 49, 54,
    56
    screen mode icons, 54
    unused space below, 53, 56
Tools menu
    Create Metadata Template
    command, 22
    Device Central command, 25

Photoshop command, 76
Tools palette, 83, 95
Tools>Cache menu, 4, 13
Tools>Photoshop menu, 112,
    126
Transfer Activation command,
    116
Transform command, 77
Transform Selection command,
    77
transformations, 101
transition effects, slideshow, 24
Transparency & Gamut section,
    Preferences dialog box, 123
Trash Can icon, 46
Trim command, 77
two-column Toolbar, 49, 54, 56
two-monitor setup, 7, 16

U

Universal Binary applications,
    124
Unsharp Mask filter, 77
Update DNG Previews
    command, 47
Use Grayscale Toolbar icon, 122
Use Legacy checkbox, 60, 79
Use Previous Layer for Clipping
    Mask checkbox, 100
Use Software Rendering setting,
    24
Use Video Alpha checkbox, 123
User Interface Brightness
    slider, 5

V

Vanishing Point dialog box,
    118–120
Vanishing Point filter, 100, 116,
    118–120
Variations adjustment, 80
vector images, 11
Version Cue, 24
Vibrance slider, 40
Video Alpha checkbox, 123
video aspect ratios, 11
video editing, 90
view icons, Bridge, 4
View menu

Refresh command, 4
Show Reject Files command,
    14
Slideshow command, 23
View/Show commands, 4
View>Sort menu, 11
Vista, Windows, 124

W

Wacom graphics tablets, 13
Welcome screen, 115
white balance icon, 17
white balance setting, 17
White Balance sliders, 28
White Point slider, 69–70
Width setting, Clone Source
    palette, 94
Window menu
    Clone Source command, 90
    Histogram command, 67
    illustrated, 50
    Info command, 66, 74
    Inspector Panel command, 24
    New Synchronized Window
    command, 6
windows, synchronizing, 6–7
Windows Vista, 124
Window>Workspace menu, 4,
    56
workflow settings, Camera Raw,
    28
Workspace menu, 4, 56

X

XML parsing support, 128
XMP files, 19, 20, 42, 46

Y

Yellows slider, 74

Z

Zoom Back and Forth setting,
    23
zoom feature, 17, 24
Zoom View command, 116
Zoomify command, 116, 125

CATCH BEN

AT

DIGITALMASTERY.COM

and get ready to say, "Aha! I finally GET Photoshop!"